MARRIED LIES

Secrets Behind Reality TV

Overcoming adversity
and discovering transformation

Married Lies
Secrets Behind Reality TV

Overcoming adversity and discovering transformation

Copyright © 2020 by Sean Thomsen

All rights reserved.

Book Cover Design: Michael Rehder

The content in this book belongs exclusively to Sean Thomsen

ISBN Paperback: 978-0-6484806-4-8_50899
ISBN Hardcover: 978-0-6484806-0-0_50899
ISBN Downloadable Audio File: 978-0-6484806-3-1_90000
ISBN EBook - EPUB: 978-0-6484806-2-4_90000
ISBN EBook – Kindle: 978-0-6484806-1-7_90000

Categories: Non-Fiction

Table of Contents

Chapter 1

Handling a Breakdown

Introduction

There's a feeling when you've been in a relationship for several months. You've had enough dates, enough talks, that you really feel you know this person. There are no more secrets. You're not on your 'best behaviour' anymore; you've let your walls down and relaxed a bit. You finally feel you can be yourself around this new person.

Now imagine you could *start* a relationship like that, or take your current relationship back to that place. Happy, confident, and 100% authentic. Imagine having the ability to deal with any situation by summoning the strength and confidence to be yourself, ask for what you want, and calmly accept the outcome.

I can show you how to overcome your limiting beliefs – that inner critic whispering, 'You're not good enough.' I can help you develop your self-knowledge and core confidence to the point that you can engage with your romantic partner or, really, anyone at all, with authenticity and unshakeable inner certainty. I can teach you how to read other people's signals through their body language and actions, so you always know what they're *really* trying to say.

I learned much of this through my experience on *Married at First Sight* in 2018, but a lot of it also came through my personal journey before and after the show. I've become an expert in self-development, both through my own study and life experience, as well as by working with coaches and mentors for years. Now I want to share what I've learned with others so you can improve your life, build your best relationship, and never settle or hide your true self ever again.

The dinner party

Have you ever had someone be so rude and aggressive towards you that you start questioning yourself, wondering if there's actually something wrong with you?

Let me tell you about the dinner party.

This was the first time that all the couples were going to meet each other on *Married at First Sight*. We had all had our weddings and honeymoons, and this was going to be our first social event. As we walked into that cocktail party, the energy in the room was electric. Months of excitement and anticipation had been building up to that point, and it felt like we were on a massive adventure. Everyone was dressed up to the nines and in high spirits, mingling and getting to know each other.

I was happy to see a contestant there from the last season – John. I went up to him and mentioned that we had a mutual friend, a contestant from the previous season. We had a bit of a chat. When the servers broke out the booze, I made a crack that they wanted to get us drunk, so we'd all start making out.

Not five minutes later, I got pulled aside for a mic check. A mic check is either a legitimate check of your microphone, or a chance for the producers to talk to you. In my case, it was the latter. Tara McWilliams, from production company Endemol Shine, had been the executive producer since season four. In the audition, she was super nice to me, so it caught me off guard to be told I shouldn't have mentioned the previous contestant or made the crack about the booze. I felt like a kid being scolded by a teacher. And I also realised right away that they were treating me differently. I wasn't the only one making jokes, but I was the only one getting yelled at for it.

My confidence took a hit, and I was a little hesitant for the rest of the evening. Other contestants were out there trying to create drama to get airtime, which they did successfully. But I wasn't interested in that game. My whole philosophy at the start was to be authentic and show my real self, and that's probably why it hurt to be criticised for it.

The next day, we had the commitment ceremony.

We were all supposed to be interviewed about our partners, our marriage so far, and whether we thought it was going to work. Then we would write down 'stay' or 'leave'. Blair and I didn't have that spark when we first met, but we were actually getting along better than most of the other couples, so I wanted to stay. It was supposed to be our choice, after all.

But one of the producers, an Endemol Shine lackey, marched into our apartment on a mission to get Blair and me to leave. It was neither love at first sight, nor a complete disaster between us, and with one or two couples storyboarded to be eliminated in the first few commitment ceremonies, we were in the firing line straightaway. Hence, the way they were speaking to us was incredibly rude and Blair was in quite a state, crying and confused.

That wasn't even the worst of it. We headed out for the taping, and every other couple had their interviews and filming, but I was segregated off with a few other guys. We had a runner watching us to make sure we didn't go anywhere, not even to stretch our legs or use the bathroom. Eventually, the other two guys who were with me were taken for their interviews, and then it was just me – all by myself in a park with a runner watching me for over an hour. I later found out they gave Blair the exact same treatment.

But I insisted I was going to stay. They couldn't make me leave; it had to be voluntary, and, considering everything I'd sacrificed to be there, I wasn't about to walk away. So they brought in the big guns.

I got a message that Tara wanted to see me in her office. She wasn't just the executive producer.

She was the person who created the vision for the show and who decided which characters were relevant and which would be taken off.

She ripped into me right away. 'What are you doing here, Sean? We don't want you here.'

I was devastated. Little did I know, that was just the start of the intimidation and bullying. I went from that ordeal straight into the commitment ceremony. When you watch the show, you can see from my body language that I was a broken man; my shoulders were hunched, and I was looking down at the ground the whole time. I tried to speak at one point but lost it and completely broke down. All my bravado was gone – all the walls I'd built to contain my insecurities failed me. My defences were stripped down and there was just raw emotion, fear and doubt.

Lean in to your low point

Imagine being at your most vulnerable, experiencing the trauma of getting attacked and broken down, and then having that broadcast all across Australia. It's had a real, significant impact on my life and relationships; I've lost friends and family members over the show and how I was portrayed. But there's always a lesson to learn. From that experience came a new, deeper confidence, and now I want to help others learn the lessons that I learned – only, without the cameras and the attacks.

The beginning of the show essentially destroyed my confidence, but there were other events leading up to that breakdown as well. Emotionally, I was in the worst state of my life and had been for some time. I had just come out of a bad breakup and started the show thinking that it would be a good experience, no matter what happened. If I met someone, great; if not, that was fine, too. Blair is a nice girl, but I knew she wasn't the girl for me; we were just too different.

I didn't have the right outlook at the time. I had thought I could handle any situation. I had read all the self-development books, been to all the seminars, travelled the world and had a lot of life experience. But I was still running on ego, and the wheels came off once I started getting berated and attacked. My fears started to surface, and I couldn't shake them off.

I started questioning myself. Why was I being treated this way? Where was this coming from? Why was I having to work harder than anyone else just to stay? My old negative self-talk came back – the feelings of self-doubt and limiting beliefs I'd had since I was a child: 'You're a failure,' 'You're a little bitch,' 'You don't deserve to be here.' They played in a loop in my mind, over and over, ripping my confidence apart.

But there was a benefit to that experience: in many ways, it was what I hoped I would get out of the show. I had forced myself to be more open, more vulnerable than I normally would be. I had allowed myself to feel those emotions of hope, and then of insecurity and fear, because I wanted to learn and grow.

When you develop your muscles with a workout, what you're actually doing is creating tiny tears in the muscle fibres. The muscle heals and builds itself back up even stronger. I wanted to do that with my confidence and my social limits: let myself get torn down and then build myself up even stronger by learning from the experience. That's what I did – and in this book, I'll show you how to do it too.

Build yourself back up

Going through the commitment ceremony and having that traumatic experience was somewhat of a blessing in disguise. A lot of self-help gurus talk about the importance of core confidence, and how to gain that inner certainty. But at that point, I was mostly running on ego, not that deep core confidence, which I will discuss in later chapters.

By exposing myself and being my authentic self throughout that commitment ceremony, I gave myself the opportunity to delve deep down inside my subconscious mind to release the burden of my past traumas and life experiences. The edited version only captures a fraction of what I actually said, and it frames that moment to look like I just had a random meltdown. Really, I was unshackling myself and growing through one of the toughest days I think I've had in my life.

Later that night and over the coming weeks, I slowly dissected that experience, mining it for learnings, discovering the ways that my deep subconscious mind shaped the events and my reactions. That's how I eventually achieved deep, identity-level change, and found the core confidence that I was after.

I'm not saying that you need to expose your raw self on national TV to do that. Instead, throughout this book, I'm going to give you guidelines to follow to find your core confidence, your belief in yourself, and your inner certainty. Armed with these tools, you'll be able to make clear-headed, confident decisions to achieve the life you want.

Discovering the power of RAS

I'll tell you about one of the most important tools I know right now.

RAS, short for Reticular Activation System, is a concept I'll call upon frequently in this book. In a nutshell, it's the idea that what you focus on becomes your reality. The brain processes 400 million bits of information, but only 2,000 bits can be processed at any given time. So, 99.9999 percent of the information that you're receiving goes unnoticed.[1] As a result, when you focus on negative things, it becomes a self-fulfilling prophecy; the negativity becomes all you see.

You can see this in action with my *Married at First Sight* experience. My breakdown was ultimately caused by me focusing on the negative – like getting blasted at the first dinner party. If I had focused on the more positive attributes of the experience, the breakdown likely wouldn't have happened.

---

1 Allan & Barbara Pease, *The Answer* (Sydney: Harlequin MIRA, 2016).

This is something I learned from a self-help teacher years ago, and it really resonated with me because it's so true. In every aspect of your life, every social interaction, every time you set a goal, you get to decide whether it's positive or negative. Ultimately, it's up to you what kinds of thoughts or feelings you're going to get out of it. Whatever you choose to focus on, you'll see more proof of...

Let me give you an example. After working in the mines for six years, I decided to buy myself a Mustang. The Mustang was just coming to Australia; no one had it yet. It was coming out as a production-line car because they had to make it for Australian specifications. So I ordered one, and suddenly, I started seeing the car everywhere – on TV, in ads, driving around on the streets. Every time I saw one, my eyes went straight for that car – I couldn't keep my eyes off it! This wasn't magic, nor a coincidence. Anything you perceive as valuable, your RAS will automatically tune into. It will become the focus, while everything else fades into the background. You can use this to your advantage by choosing to focus on the things you want in your life. With RAS, those positive things really can become your reality.

Chapter 2

A Rolling Stone

We can all remember that time in our lives when we were young, with our future ahead of us, and it felt like the sky was the limit. One thing I'm here to tell you is that you can have that feeling back at any time of life. Just because you might be settled in a relationship or a job, doesn't mean you have to stay that way. The empowering truth is, you can decide to try for something better, or even just something different, anytime you want.

Have you ever heard the proverb 'A rolling stone gathers no moss'? It has two meanings. The first one is that if you keep moving from one place to another, you'll never prosper. That was definitely the prevailing belief when I was growing up in Brisbane. It was a given in my family and social circles that you would start work as soon as you could, earn a minimum wage, settle down young and have a family. We knew from an early age exactly how our lives were supposed to unfold: just like everyone else's. The emphasis was on stability, security and, above all, not taking a risk. There's nothing wrong with this life – it suits a lot of people. There's honour in working nine to five and being a family man. But, even back then, I knew I didn't want that for my future. I wanted to grow; I wanted to know more and *be* more at thirty-five than I was at twenty-five.

But remember, I said the proverb has *two* meanings. Being a 'rolling stone' actually sounds like a pretty good thing these days. First, the Rolling Stones made it cool, and now we have the modern idea that you *should* keep moving, keep learning and growing and experiencing new things, all through your life.

That's how I started my self-improvement journey in 2006. I was working in a job I didn't particularly like, as a trade assistant at a convention centre in Brisbane. It was a minimum-wage job and very boring. The crew was small, so we all got to know one another and shared our stories. I realised that many of my co-workers had a lot of regret about not taking more chances. One afternoon, I was sitting with another trade assistant, Mark, sorting nuts and bolts. At one point, he looked up at me and said, 'This is what you've got to look forward to.' You can imagine how that sounded to me as a twenty-something. This was all I'd ever do with my life, for twenty or thirty years? Sort nuts and bolts?

A few months later, Mark was diagnosed with late-stage cancer. Doctors gave him twelve months to live and sent him for chemotherapy. I'll never forget that he came back to work, the dedicated family man wanting to earn and provide, a week after finishing chemo. The next week, he passed away.

We went to the funeral and I remember the speeches as Mark's family spoke about his life and achievements. They touched on his love of sports and affectionately referred to him as 'a bit of a couch potato'. It was clear he'd lived a life of commitment to his family and his job. But I couldn't say I wanted my life to look the same.

Around this time, I went through a bad breakup. My girlfriend and I had been together for a while and had just moved in together when she dumped me out of nowhere on my birthday. I never saw it coming. Before I knew it, I was single and moving back in with my parents, in my mid-twenties. Between the breakup and losing my co-worker, Mark, to cancer, I felt like I was at a tipping point – ready for a massive change.

After the breakup, I realised how little I really knew about relationships and interacting with other people. I'd always found it difficult to socialise in certain groups when I was younger, and that anxiety came bubbling up again. But, this time, I felt there must be a way to get better. Lots of people were shy when they were young and then became more social later on. There must be a way for me to improve myself – read up, practise, and form the right habits.

I started researching self-development and taking Tony Robbins books into work with me to read in the storeroom. After all, if I was going to improve myself, I was going to do it during work hours! Those first few books showed me that I had a lot to learn about social skills and self-development. As I studied, I realised there was a whole world out there that I didn't know about.

There were schools of thought, skills and beliefs I had never even heard of – but which I really wanted to learn. I started to expand my horizons in terms of what I thought was possible for my life.

Finding the dating community

After taking some online courses, I found my way into a community of speakers who were giving talks about dating and confidence, and I attended a few seminars. Of course, there are some aspects of the dating community that can be really toxic. I wasn't looking to manipulate or take advantage of anyone. I just knew that I really needed to learn things like confidence, self-awareness and how to relate to people, and in this community, there were people willing to teach me those skills.

In fact, I was lucky enough that James, one of my friends from Brisbane, was in the self-help industry, so I reached out to him. If you're willing to open yourself up, people are often more than happy to help.

James taught at boot camps about dating and how to pick up women. I became his unofficial apprentice, going along with him to events and soaking up as much information as I could. It was almost like doing a university degree in improving myself! I knew it wasn't going to be something that happened in a few weeks or even months. I was in it for the long haul. If you want to make significant changes in your life, it can take years to build up those skills, especially when it comes to interacting, socialising, reading people and picking up on social dynamics. You need to test your limits and find your blind spots by putting yourself in awkward situations, so you can tweak and improve your approach accordingly.

I learned so much by working alongside this dating coach. I was also completing an apprenticeship to learn a trade, and I was gaining life experience and confidence from that. By then, I had the confidence, social skills, and earning ability to go anywhere I wanted and meet people. Why not put myself out there? So, that's exactly what I did – I went all out. I travelled the world with James and helped out at his seminars, and I got so good at meeting and dating girls naturally, my ego soared to astronomical heights. I became so addicted to the constant validation, that I did and said whatever I wanted.

As I got more girls and more validation, I kept waiting for that sense of ease and abundance to hit. I kept waiting to feel comfortable, relaxed and happy with everything I had achieved. But, finally, I realised something unexpected: I didn't feel any different as a successful adult than I did as an awkward kid or an insecure twenty-something. All the external validation in the world couldn't change it. I still had that inner voice from my childhood telling me, 'You're still a little piece of shit.'

I would try arguing with the inner voice by pointing to the tangible evidence of my success. 'Look at all these things I have! The bank account... the girls... Don't you see, inner voice? They love me!' I pushed harder and harder... which brings us back to the reunion backlash that burst the bubble that was my life. In the blink of an eye, I lost it all. The validation quickly turned to hate, my 'friends' disowned me, my bank account was wiped out, and I gained a grotesque amount of weight from stress eating and drinking.

As clichéd as it sounds, it was in that moment of losing everything that I found everything. During that backlash, I started the first steps to what would become an insane amount of deep inner work. I was on a journey to discover how I could possibly bounce back from this 'knockout blow' and why my success before the scandal never made me feel fulfilled. I unearthed every hard-written childhood trauma and bullshit egotistical belief. I strip-mined my subconscious, leaving nothing but the truth.

Get moving

Through this whole journey, I've learned that helping people, having empathy, and caring for people is my calling. And that's what I've tried to do ever since.

So here's my first piece of advice to someone who wants to change their life: the key is just to take a first step, however small. My first step was finding self-help books and reading them in spare moments at work. I didn't spend a lot of money or quit my job or anything dramatic. But that small change was enough leverage to start my life moving in a different direction. And then I started to pick up momentum from there. I became a rolling stone, single-minded and unstoppable.

You don't even need to know exactly what kind of life you want; just get started doing something different, something to improve yourself. For now, just think about one or two new habits you could start to build. There's no telling how far it can take you. In the next chapter, I'll explain how to set goals effectively and achieve them with the power of RAS.

Chapter 3
The Power of Goal Setting

My goal to move cities

Post *Married at First Sight*, I needed a fresh start – that's why I decided to move to Melbourne. While this wasn't a massive goal, it's a good example of all the steps you need to go through to complete a goal.

The first thing I did was write down *exactly* what I wanted to achieve: *Live in Melbourne by the end of this year.* I put that note in my wallet, where I'd see it every time I opened it. Now, this wasn't a particularly practical goal. I owned property in Perth. Any business expert, or even friend, would have told me to just stay put. But I knew Melbourne offered opportunities for me to *grow* my business, not just maintain it. That was a gamble worth taking.

So I thought through the steps I would have to take to accomplish my goal – even without knowing whether I could succeed in the end or not. I thought, 'I want to move to Melbourne. It might be a long shot; but what would it take to do it? Well, to start, I'd need to rent out my place and find a new one in Melbourne.' So I decided to actually give it a try, call a real estate agent, and see what happened.

I still didn't know how I was going to pull it off, as the real estate market at that particular time was horrible. Even just renting out my property was going to be an ordeal. But I kept my goal to move to Melbourne at the forefront of my mind constantly. Every time I opened my wallet, I had to look at the note where I had written it down. Then, all of a sudden, unexpected opportunities in Melbourne started to arise. I contacted the real estate agent and, within a couple of weeks, I had someone saying they wanted to move into my place. Sometimes, a bit of luck plays into your hands. But it wasn't just luck; I had also built friendships that came in handy. The same evening I arrived in Melbourne, I was able to call up my brother and stay at his place.

But the crucial thing is that I set this goal and then started looking around for ways to make it work. I also built a team of people to help me reach that goal: people like the real estate agent and my friends. I called, told them what I was trying to do, and asked for their help. If I hadn't set that goal, as unrealistic as it looked at first, I wouldn't have looked out for those resources, and they wouldn't have come through like they did.

That's an important part of accomplishing your goals – knowing how to outsource the work and build your team. Once you speak your goal to someone else and ask for their help, it becomes real. And now, that person will follow-up with you and hold you accountable, if only in a small way. Now you're not the only one driving this goal forward: others are going to contribute their energy and help you gain momentum.

Even so, the experience wasn't without its setbacks, the following story illustrates some of the obstacles you might encounter towards achieving your goals.It's a brisk Thursday morning. I had one thought racing in my mind over and over: *What's the worst that could happen? It's only been there for a few days.* I quickly dart across the airport foyer in search of a taxi. Luckily, this time there's no line. I jump into the back of the taxi, a little bit anxious because of the phone call I had received a few days beforehand.

'Mr Thomsen, do you own a Ford Mustang?' the woman said, and told me she was a police constable.

'Why, yes,' I answered.

'Well, it's currently parked at the casino car park, and we're just wondering when you're going to reclaim it?'

'Oh, sorry, Constable. Yes. I was just staying at the casino, and I've been called away to work for a couple of days.' But I was thinking, *Jesus, I only left the car parked there for a few days and they're harassing me already. God, these guys are onto it... I suppose I really do need to move the car.*

When the constable started speaking again, I said: 'Well, I've actually got a reservation there as soon as I get back. It's already booked.' I thought: *There – that should get them off my back!*

Then I said: 'So, I'm going to be back there tomorrow morning. So, if you guys could just leave the car where it is, I'm checking back into the casino then, and leaving the next day to drive to Melbourne.'

She interrupted me: 'Security say they're gonna get this thing towed, but as long as you're back tomorrow morning, that should be okay. I'll just double-check with them, but I'm sure it will be fine.'

'Thank you again, Constable,' I said, but I was actually thinking: *My car getting towed is the last thing I need. It's fully packed with my suitcases, camera gear, all the knickknacks from the apartment ready for the drive to Melbourne. Jesus, it's just one more night. What? What's the worst that can happen?*

Then I get into the taxi and the cabby is in an unusually friendly mood. He keeps on trying to generate conversation with me.

'It's a wonderful day, isn't it? Do you work in the mines? What do you do?'

'Is it 50-million-question day?' I snapped back. 'Do you know where the casino is? I need to get there quickly. Just go down the highway and kind of step on it, mate. I have a gut feeling something's wrong.'

'What do you mean?' he asks.

'Ah, I left my car parked at the casino; I had to race back to work for a couple of days.'

'Oh, that carport is under constant CCTV monitoring, so you shouldn't have any issues there. You shouldn't have any issues.'

'Well, thanks for reassuring me, but I've just been worried. I've got to call off the police. They said that security had contacted them about a car being parked there for over three days. But I was just checked-in there. Surely they would have monitored the fact that I was checked-in there? And I gave them my rego number, so they must've, soon as I'd checked out, got straight onto me. I'm like, *Man, where can I find the luck?'*

The cabbie then says: 'Well, I'm hoping the best for you, sir. Anyway, we'll be there in about ten minutes.'

As we're getting closer, I start getting a bit clammy in the hands. Just had this gut feeling – churning, thinking about all the stuff that I had in my car. If that were to get broken into, god, it'd just be absolutely devastating.

So we arrive at the car park and I direct him right to where my car is. As we pull up, I look at him and I'm like, 'I don't have a good feeling about this.'

He's like, 'Ah, I'm sure it'll be fine. They have security guards there – we see a security guard riding around on his pushbike and that's 24/7.'

I'm like, 'Yeah, true, true. That's right.'

We pull up to the car. I walk around suspiciously. Around the side of the car, I can kind of see some glass shattered on the floor. As I continue to walk, I start getting more anxious. I'm edging closer. I can see the glass on the floor and I'm like, *Oh, no.* I walk over to the driver's side entrance and there's glass littered all over the driver's seat, all over the floor, and all my bags have been ripped through. It looks like a jackal has been released in the back seat: bags torn open, clothes strewn everywhere.

My heart sinks. Then I see that the nice constable slapped a bright orange abandoned-vehicle sticker on the passenger side window. It's a fucking open invitation. I'm like, *Huh, maybe this is a sign from God. Maybe I shouldn't go on this bloody trip. I can't catch a break. I've left the car here for one extra night and look what's happened.*

To my astonishment, I see a ripe apple core on my car roof, just above the broken window. This fucking arsehole who robbed me was casually just eating an apple. I'm like, *Ah, that's good. He's just had a nice little bite of his apple, smashed the window, and started taking all my shit out.* I couldn't believe it.

After that initial angst and worry, I start getting really, really fucking enraged, because, at that moment, I see one of the security patrols zip past on his bike. This guy's literally 15 metres away, just riding his pushbike casually past my car. I'm like, 'Oi, mate!'

'Yes, sir. Can I help you?' he says.

'Yeah, mate. Can you see what's wrong here with this picture?'

'Let me have a look, sir.'

'The whole fucking window is smashed in and all my shit's gone. I'm fucking staying here tonight. Do you actually look at the cars or are you picturing riding in the Tour de France – what the fuck?'

The security guy gets defensive. 'Well, there's a big area to cover, sir, so we can't constantly patrol the same spot.'

I'm like, 'Look, man, there's a security camera just over there. Surely you can bring it up and find out who the fuck stole all my shit?'

'Ah, yes, sir, we'll definitely do that,' he says.

After that initial angst, a wave of anger washes over me, just thinking about all the repercussions.

'Look, I can't drive a car across Australia with a fucking broken window. How am I going to recoup all this stuff that I've lost? I don't even know what I've lost at this point. I've got all my work stuff in there. I've got laptops. I've got other important paperwork that one needs. I can't believe this just happened to me!'

I started refocusing on the whole trip. *No. I need to be in the right frame of mind. I need to start moving forward. Look, it's not a big deal. Start taking a couple of deep breaths. Breathe in for a count of four. Exhale. Breathe in. It's only stuff. I can get it back. Breathe out. Okay, Sean. It's not a big deal. Let's just do what we can.*

So I took action – straight on the phone to the insurance company. 'Okay. I've got my car here. I need a tow truck here within the hour to come pick it up.'

'Don't worry, sir. We'll see if we can get someone there as soon as possible,' they say.

Okay, great, I'm thinking. *Onto that. Now I need someone to repair the window.* So I call up a window repair place. Boom.

'Do you have a spare window for a driver's side Mustang?'

'Yes, sir. You're in luck. This is our last one. We can get it on the window by tomorrow morning.'

'Great, because I've got to start driving to Melbourne that day,' I say.

'It'll only take a couple of hours, sir, so that'd be fine.'

Awesome. Look, shit's starting to work out already. It's fine. It's all a matter of perception, just take a couple of deep breaths. It's not the end of the world.

As soon as I get the car towed, I pick up my bags and walk into the casino.

'Good evening, sir. Checking in?'

'Yeah, I'm checking in.'

Despite all that, part of what helped me keep going was the fact that I had already set things in motion. I had put a deposit on a place in Melbourne; I had a move-in date and a lease waiting for me. Those deadlines helped keep me on track, because I had commitments to keep.

The lesson here is, don't be afraid to make concrete commitments on your way to your goal. It can feel scary at the time, especially when it involves money, like my deposit. But those commitments will help keep you motivated when you most need to be.

The biggest misconceptions about goals

1. Fear is bad

While many people think of fear as a negative thing, I believe it can actually be a powerful instigator of change in your life. Whether it's being in a bad relationship or stuck in a dead-end job you hate, it can be really helpful to project your current life into the future. If you do nothing, what will your life look like next year? In three years? Five years?

Really take the time to visualise what your future will look like if you stay on your current track – in great detail. Close your eyes and take yourself on a tour of your potential future. Where do you live? Who's next to you when you wake up? How do you spend your morning? Your workday? How do you feel when you get home from work? How does your evening unfold? Imagine each of these steps in vivid detail... That's what you can expect, if you don't take any steps to change your future.

As you take yourself through this process, do you feel a growing sense of fear or concern? Good. Use it. That fear can help you avoid complacency. Leverage that fear to help you work up the nerve to make a difficult change. Get yourself to the point where you feel like even if you try and fail, you'll still be better off. That's a powerful position to be in if you want change in your life.

2. You're not in control

Another common misconception many people have is that they have no control over their life and future, that it's all predetermined. You might believe you're stuck in your job or relationship, or that it's all you deserve. Even if you believe you *could* change, it's easy to feel like it's too hard or you're too busy. You can get so buried in your day-to-day activities that you don't feel you have the energy to pursue a change. But really what's happening is, you're taking an 'out of sight, out of mind' approach to your goals. Once a year, you might write down New Year's resolutions or one-, three- or five-year goals, but then you put the list away and never look at it again.

That's why, once you've resolved to make a change, you need to make sure those goals stay front of mind. You'd be surprised how things seem to just come together to help you get where you want to go once you've clearly decided where that is. People call this 'the power of the universe' and it sounds airy-fairy. But it's true: what you focus on tends to come to life.

Getting started: make it concrete

When you're envisioning a new goal, the first thing to do is make it real to yourself. Most goals start off as daydreams, and if you're not careful, that's what they'll stay. What you want to do is bring that goal into the real world. Make it concrete. Tell people about it; write it down; have an accountability buddy like some people do with their weight-loss goals – whatever it takes so that you don't forget it. You need to make sure your goal stays at the forefront of your mind as much as possible.

Writing down your goals and reading them out at least once a day is also how you program your subconscious mind and direct your RAS. With your goal at the top of your mind, you will naturally start to find ways to achieve it, even when you're not directly thinking about it. So you need to be constantly thinking about what you want to achieve, otherwise, it just fades into the background as you get caught up in the daily grind.

Another way you can do this is by writing out a list of your main goals (these should be no more than ten words each) on a post-it note and keep them in your wallet.[2] That way, you can revisit your goals every day and you're always subconsciously thinking about your goals and how you're going to achieve them. This is a realistic approach to actually sticking to your goals.

Constantly revisit and refine your approach

The next part of accomplishing your goals is revisiting and refining them. Every step that you take towards your goal is a chance to collect feedback and see if you need to make any adjustments. The bigger the goal, the longer you'll spend trying to accomplish it, and the more check-ins you'll need to make sure you're still on track.

Take career goals. Do you remember what you wanted to be when you were a kid? How often have you changed, refined and adjusted that goal over the years?

Some goals aren't as simple as moving cities; sometimes, the thing we want to change is ourselves. But change – particularly to yourself – doesn't come easily, so think of it as a long-term goal. That means you need to be constantly assessing where you're at, taking in feedback, and adjusting your approach.

---

2   Richard Parkes Cordock, *Millionaire Upgrade: Lessons in success from those who travel at the sharp end of the plane* (Chichester: Capstone, 2006)

My self-improvement goal – fix my grades

College never came easily to me, and my grades weren't impressive. When I was in class, I always struggled to concentrate. My mind would dart around, and I could never focus on the task at hand. So I had to set a goal to get better at college.

I decided to figure out what I needed to do to be successful despite my limitations. Eventually, I decided that, to compensate for my short attention span, I needed to over-prepare. If we had an exam, I couldn't just cram the night before, like my friends did; I needed at least two or three weeks to prepare. Whatever I thought the normal expectations were to prepare for something, I would always put in the extra mile – or two.

Then, I was constantly revisiting my approach and making marginal adjustments and improvements. If I did well on a test, I'd try to figure out what I did that was working. And the same if I did poorly – I'd try to figure out what I could improve on for next time. I didn't waste any time feeling sorry for myself or feeling that it wasn't 'fair' that I had to work harder than my peers; I just did what worked for me, even if it meant working harder. The question to ask yourself is, 'How badly do I want to succeed? What would it take? Am I willing to put in the effort?'

Goal setting is the same sort of thing. Know your strengths and limitations, make a plan that caters to your strengths, and figure out what you need to do to overcome your weaknesses. Try things out and see whether they work or not – find something to improve or change for next time.

What not to do – my career goal

Sometimes, you start off with a particular goal, and once you achieve it, you realise you actually wanted something different. How do you avoid putting in all that work just to find that you still don't have the thing you really want?

A critical technique for this is visualisation, as I mentioned at the top of the chapter. This time, imagine what it will feel like once you've achieved your goal. Close your eyes and imagine your perfect day from start to finish, in as much detail as you can. Where do you live? When you wake up, who's next to you? How do you spend your morning? Do you work, and if so, what do you do? What do you do in the evening?

I knew from an early age that I wanted to make good money. I grew up in a blue-collar environment and it was a given that you would have to work hard to earn money; the more money you wanted to make, the harder and longer you had to work. Working wasn't seen as enjoyable or fulfilling. There wasn't much talk about following your passion. Work was a hard slog and you did it for the money.

So, I started working as a trade assistant. It was physical work, and the pay wasn't great. I knew I wanted a better life, but at the time, I just thought that meant making more money. I didn't know then, as I was young, what a better life could really look like. So, I figured I needed a job that paid better, and I didn't care what it took.

This was just as the mining boom was taking off, and it was all anyone was talking about. Everyone knew two things: mining jobs paid really well, and it was really hard to get one. But I was laser-focused and didn't care what I had to do. To finish my apprenticeship, I took a job that I absolutely hated by the end. I moved around the east coast of Australia finding jobs that would help me get mining experience: Newcastle, Sydney and, finally, WA. For my first mining job, I worked a rotating shift: four weeks on, one week off.

Now, mining jobs are a mixed bag. There are jobs that really wear you down, and that's sort of where I started. What I really needed was to target my desired outcome in terms of work-life balance. There are good mining jobs that allow you to have that; you just need to look for them.

But I didn't know that then. When the first pay cheque landed in my bank account, it felt amazing. I had achieved my goal – I was making the kind of money I had been craving. Over time, I started to realise that the way I was working wasn't worth it. I didn't have the work-life balance I wanted.

See, I hadn't dug deeper into my goal to find out what I really wanted. When I said to myself, 'I want to make more money,' what I really meant was, 'I want a life with passion and drive; I want to have a sense of greater purpose instead of just worrying about survival.' But I hadn't taken the time to visualise what my life would be like.

I ended up accomplishing what I set out to do, but not getting what I really wanted, so I had to go back and adjust my goal. I targeted a change of roster and title that would get me that work-life balance I was looking for.

It's not uncommon to have to change goals; in fact, it's a normal part of the process. However, it helps to be aware that what you want and what you *think* you want aren't always the same. That way, you'll be prepared to change course when needed.

So, my advice to you is, start by imagining how your life will look once you get where you want to go. Find out the details: if it's a job you're after, what is it really like to work that job? Will you still want to be there five or ten years from now? What is it that you *really* want? On the surface, I wanted more money, but beneath that, what I really wanted was freedom – and if I had known that, I would have known that I shouldn't settle for just any job. I would have been able to set a real goal, to build the life I really wanted.

Chapter 4

The Art of Storytelling

If you want a conversation to go your way, you need to become a great storyteller. Think of some of the people you enjoy spending time with. What do you like about them? Chances are, it comes down to storytelling. A job interview is just an opportunity for you to tell a story about your career that will convince the hiring manager to hire you. A date is an opportunity for you to tell a story about who you are and what you're looking for. Learn how to become a captivating storyteller, and you will gain the ability to influence your audience to get the result you want.

Jordan Belfort, the Wolf of Wall Street, wrote that when you're talking to a client, you have four seconds to establish that you're sharp as a tack, energetic as hell, and an expert in your field. The same goes for telling a great story or having a great conversation: you need to know the effect you want to have on your audience, and be prepared to tell the right story, the right way, to get that result.

When you strike up a conversation with someone new, you need to be prepared to practice the 90/10 rule. Because you've initiated the conversation, you need to be willing to speak 90 percent of the time. That's not to say that you necessarily *need* to speak 90 percent of the time, but you must be prepared to do so, if required. By keeping the desired outcome in mind, you have the power to keep the conversation moving in the right direction.

How to tell a great story

Legend has it there are only seven universal plotlines in the world, and every story ever told fits into one of them. But some say it all boils down to one: the hero's journey. In the hero's journey, we meet a seemingly ordinary boy or girl living an ordinary life. One day, that life is interrupted – a problem pops up or someone new comes in. Because of this interruption, the hero goes on a quest and comes back with new powers to help his/her fellow man.

Every myth, folktale and anecdote can be described with this one structure. The fastest way to become a captivating storyteller is to access that universal structure by including three key elements:

1. **The situation**: The who, what, where, when, why and how.
2. **The interruption:** This is the crescendo of your story – some kind of tension, drama or obstacle to the situation.

3. **The solution**: How the situation was resolved or any changes that occurred as a result.

When it comes to telling an engaging story, preparation is key. It's a good idea to have the story ready to go in your mind and you can always expand on certain aspects as you go. The way to make your audience more interested in particular parts of your story (for example, the interruption or drama) is to amp up the level of detail. For example, whenever I'm asked about how I started the process for getting on *Married at First Sight*, I have a story ready to go that I've perfected over the past year or two. It's a story about how you go from being a regular guy with a normal life to appearing on a reality show. And it starts with a phone call.

It came while I was at work, on a typical summer day.

'Hi, this is Sarah from *Married at First Sight* casting. Are you still interested in applying?'

I was completely confused. Still interested? I didn't even remember applying!

'You filled out the first page of the form several months ago, so I'm just inquiring if you are still interested.'

Oh, *that* form. Now I remembered. Months ago, I found the website and started filling out the online application form on a whim. I got through the first page, and then realised the form was way longer than I'd thought. I couldn't be bothered with all that, so I just exited out of the site without finishing and forgot all about it.

My first thought was, *I can't do the show. I'm not even single!* But that reminded me of how weird things had been lately between me and the girl I was seeing. I had deep feelings for her, but we had just come out of the honeymoon phase and I was starting to suspect we weren't going to make it. We had started off so well, feeling completely in love and even thinking about settling down and starting a family. But then I left for my next work rotation, and when I got back, things had changed. She'd moved her attention to other guys and she wasn't being honest with me. Much as part of me wanted to make it work, I was starting to come to terms with the fact that it wasn't going to last. Besides, what were the chances I would actually get on to the show?

So, I made the decision. 'Yeah, I'm interested,' I told Sarah.

'Okay, cool,' she said. 'Can we set up a Skype call in a few days? We just want to get a sense of who you are, your background, your history.'

'Absolutely,' I said.

And that was the start of my journey through the audition process to get cast on *Married at First Sight.*

Months later, I'd finally done and sent them everything they asked for and all I could do was wait to hear back. It had been weeks with no word. Nick had heard back for his season in August, and we were in September now. Maybe it wasn't happening. I tried to be ready for rejection, but really I was hoping so hard to get in. They'd put so much time into this process. Surely they wouldn't do that if they weren't interested?

I was at the airport, at the end of my work rotation, waiting to fly back to Perth. The phone rang. They had found me a match. They wanted to set up the wedding in two weeks. Holy shit!

I told my co-workers about it and we celebrated with beers at the airport. It was a really exciting moment. Then I had to scramble to get an entire wedding organised, with suits, a best man, speeches, everything. The crew showed up to film my backstory piece; they got shots of me driving my Mustang, getting coffee with my mates, doing a gym session with my personal trainers. It was a really fun experience – a little stressful because of the wedding coming up, but the camera crew and producer were super nice. I remember thinking, *If it's all like this, I'm going to have a ball!*

Of course, it wasn't all like that; not at all. But that's a different story.

All the details in that story: the phone calls, the anticipation… that's how you draw people into your story and keep them on the edge of their seats. Also, note how that story follows the hero's journey structure: it starts by setting the scene in my regular life, then shows how the audition process interrupted that, and builds up towards this moment of anticipation. Even though you know how the story ends, it still captures your imagination because the details pull you in and get you feeling that anxiety and anticipation that we've all felt before.

Of course, it's not just about the story itself – it's also about how you *tell* the story. To be an engaging storyteller, you need to nail your vocal tonality. The way you speak can have a huge impact on how the message is communicated and received – this is what neuro-linguistic programming is all about.

There are three different levels of vocal tonality, each with different outcomes. Once you understand these tonalities, you'll know how to use just the tone of your voice to get what you want.

Rapport: A high-pitched, upward inflection. For example, a door-to-door salesperson asking you how your day has been. This pitch tends to establish rapport by implying a need or request.

Neutral: Fairly flat and level, with neither an upward nor downward inflection. Most commonly used in everyday conversations and small talk.

Dominance: A low, sharp and downward inflection, achieving a slightly aggressive or assertive tone.

I witnessed firsthand how vocal tonality was used to achieve certain outcomes on the set of *Married at First Sight*. If the producers wanted to provoke a certain reaction from a contestant, they would break the rapport to assert dominance. It would make you feel like a little schoolkid in trouble if you weren't aware of what they were doing! Their whole job is to manipulate contestants and neuro-linguistic programming plays a big part in how they do that.

The audition and storytelling

I believe storytelling played an important role in nailing my *Married at First Sight* audition and scoring a spot on the show. One of the biggest mistakes people make when auditioning is trying to live up to the people they've seen on reality shows before. They think 'I'm going to be really loud and energetic,' because they've seen other contestants with wild and crazy personalities. But people in the television industry are very good at reading people and can see right through the facade.

Most of the time, they just want sincere people who can convey their message with confidence. Think of it like trying to pick someone up. You want someone genuine who you can have a conversation with, because it puts you at ease, right? The same goes for the audition process. Whatever gimmick you think is going to be your ticket into the show, scrap it and just be as authentic as possible.

I went into the process at an interesting time, because I had just come out of a painful breakup. So, in the audition, I told them the story of how my relationship ended. There was no hiding behind a filter or putting on a persona. I just allowed myself to be real and raw as I relived those painful moments in my story. Because I allowed myself to be an open book, the producers connected with my story and felt compassion for me.

Sometimes on these reality shows, they can film you for twelve hours straight. No persona is going to hold up to that. You're going to end up showing every side of yourself: happy Sean, sad Sean, angry Sean. So, obviously, in the audition, they ask you different questions to trigger different responses. I just made sure to answer in a completely honest and authentic way, like when they asked me upfront how many people I had slept with, and I answered honestly. It wasn't the number they were impressed with, but the fact that I was so open answering the question.

In those situations, you need to play up your genuine attributes – these are the things that are going to give you and your story the edge over the competition. My thing was being as honest and authentic as possible – people tend to respect and gravitate towards that. They knew they were dealing with the real me, not just an act I was putting on for the audition.

The other thing I believe got me over the line was confidence. I wasn't attached to the outcome of the audition; in fact, since I had just come out of a bad breakup, I wasn't interested in much of anything. I think that emotional distance actually helped me, because I wasn't overly eager to please, and I didn't come off as desperate. Part of the art of storytelling is not being overly invested in what your audience will think of you. For example, one useful technique is to tell a self-deprecating story about a time you did something stupid. But if you're worried about what the audience will think of you, you won't want to go there. You'll be too afraid of what people will think and you won't want to be that vulnerable. But knowing how to be vulnerable is how you can charm and disarm people.

Any time you're walking into a conversation and you have a specific outcome that you want, it's best to try to put that out of your mind. Tell yourself you don't much care either way and – ironically – that will give you the confidence you need to be successful.

Part of that confidence also comes from believing you're ready. Recall everything you've been through and remind yourself that this new attempt fits perfectly into your life experience. Have faith in yourself. When I walked into that audition, I knew with a hundred-percent confidence that I was going to get it. It felt like everything else I had been through had been leading up to this – I had gone through a trial by fire and nothing could shake me, whether I got in or not.

Another important thing to remember when it comes to reality TV is that you need to be prepared for fallout. Even if you're being a hundred-percent authentic, they are casting for certain characters and they're going to play that up in editing. Are you prepared to potentially be cast as the bad guy? Are you mentally strong enough to deal with people sending you nasty messages or yelling at you on the street, when they don't actually know you? Probably half the cast knew exactly what they were in for and the rest of us had no idea. I think the producers liked that we were so green, because they could manipulate us and get us to do certain things we wouldn't normally do.

So, would I go through the experience again? It depends which day you ask me! Sometimes, it seems life would be a lot easier if I hadn't done it; but, then, I wouldn't have had the opportunities that have made me grow as a person.

Chapter 5

Situational vs. Core Confidence

The two things people understand the least about themselves is how loved they are and how much damage they cause by not believing it.

I'm going to tell you a cautionary tale.

This story is about a guy so insecure, so consumed by anger, that he created a plan to get revenge on the producers of a reality show who fucked him over.

Okay , it's a story about me. But I'm not proud of it. I'm telling it to show how destructive a lack of confidence can be.

When I was booted from *Married at First Sight*, I was so bitter and angry that I decided to take over the reunion show and make it all about me. That would be my revenge on the producers who sidelined me and made me feel like garbage.

When I set my mind to something, I don't care what it takes or how it will make me look. To make sure I'd be the centre of attention at the reunion show, I decided that I was going to systematically hook up with every viable girl who had been on the show. Good idea, Sean! Everyone was back at home I knew I had roughly two months now that the season was over, and I thought about who I could easily get to from Perth. Tracey lived in Perth, but she beat me to the punch, asking me to grab drinks and catch up. She was perceived as the victim on the show, and it played beautifully into her hands.

On the show, when Dean said no to the relationship at the first commitment ceremony, it set the precedent for her to play the victim, which she certainly did. She knew how to play it to the full extent, maximising sympathy from the audience for how she'd been wronged by Dean, by him having sex with her the morning of the commitment ceremony then going on to say no to the relationship. It was all in her favour from the outset, which allowed her to play well to her strengths.

She was surprisingly keen to meet up. I picked her up from her place and we went for drinks. She was heavily flirting with me. It did feel good not to be the one having to do all the pursuing. After a couple of drinks, we went back to my place...

They always say, if it seems too good to be true, it probably is. Well, Tracey was too good to be true. She paid for everything. Dinners, drinks – she even booked us a trip to Bali staying in a $1000-a-night villa. The compensation was that she kept the thousands from the media 'paparazzi' sales from when we were dating – a fair trade. At the time, I thought she was trying to buy my love. With hindsight, I realise it was simpler: she wanted to be famous and thought our relationship would help. Both of us were really just using each other.

By the time we got to the reunion filming, Tracey had been whispering in my ear for weeks about Dean. It seemed Dean had some background in the media world, so he knew how to pretty much get the show revolving around him from the start. That's why, at the initial commitment ceremony, he said no to the relationship and made up some pretty flimsy excuses as to why he was saying no, just to create that controversy and drama. That's also why I played into Tracey's hands so well.

Dean works in production, so he knew exactly what the producers were looking for. He and Tracey had this seesawing relationship throughout the whole show. When Dean finally, at the end of the show, confessed his undying love for Tracey, and Tracey said no, it played out perfectly. Tracey told me after the show that they had both planned to say yes, but for that added bit of drama, Tracey said no and it backfired on Dean, which he didn't expect.

But Dean kept on adding fuel to the fire by sending racy text messages to Tracey, and Tracey... well, she told me she wasn't reciprocating, though probably, with hindsight, she was. So I only got her side of the story. And, by then, I was so jaded by the whole process that no relationship would ever, ever have come out of the show.

Then it came to the day of the reunion. I knew something big was going to happen – I could feel it. Just by what I was wearing, I knew that I'd get some attention. But I was out to prove a point that

I couldn't be manipulated, that I couldn't be kept quiet. I was extremely nervous – I remember that. But there was also an underlying energy; they had us all segregated off in white tents, in this big warehouse. Half of it was backstage where they isolated all the participants and the other half was the actual live production area where they had the cocktail area and the adjoining dinner room.

I managed to smuggle in a couple of small bottles of vodka, like you get on planes. Once it was closer to the start of the reunion, I sculled the vodka and washed it down with lukewarm coffee. I went out to the reunion area on my own, separate from Tracey, because the producers wanted to downplay the whole relationship. But Dean obviously knew that I had come there with intentions, and he knew what kind of buttons to push. Dean 'made a beeline for Tracey, found his opportunity to sit next to her, and then started commenting on how good she looked, and how they could still be really good friends.

In the weeks leading up to the reunion, Tracey had been saying to me how much she despised Dean. I don't know if she was doing it intentionally – maybe she knew that I would react to it on the night. I'm not sure if she really was planning that much ahead, but that's how it initially escalated. And, of course, later on in the night, once everyone was heavily liquored, the producers hit up Dean to go grab me for another chat – knowing that nothing good would come from that conversation, and that it would only escalate the drama for the circus that was the dinner party.

So between that scenario and my anger over how the producers treated me, I was ready for anything. That's where the fight between Dean and I came from. But that fight really wasn't about Dean at all; Dean was just out to create drama, the same as the rest of us. I didn't really have anything against him. But whenever I thought about the treatment I got from the producers, I was white with rage. That anger that you see, in my fight with Dean, is really meant for the producers.

In the end, I got my wish; both parts of the reunion show focused on me. But there was a huge cost. The backlash was out of this world. I got hate-posts, death threats, you name it, through social media – thousands of posts and messages over a few days. It was overwhelming. What confidence I had left, fell to pieces. I couldn't deal with everything that was coming at me.

Over the following months, I went on a journey to learn about myself and build a new identity. Since then, I feel I've completely changed as a person. This happens to a lot of people who go through something traumatic, particularly something involving public hatred. They come out the other side, and they're completely changed.

We've all heard of post-traumatic stress disorder. But have you ever heard of post-traumatic growth? It's not a health condition. It's an outcome that researchers have noticed, and they're still working to try to explain it. Typically, when someone goes through something traumatic and receives psychological counselling or therapy, the goal of the therapy is to get them back to 'normal' – meaning, how they were before. Same job, same friends, same personality, same routine. If you do, you're considered to have successfully recovered. If not, they figure you're not there yet. But researchers have noticed that some patients behave differently. They don't go back to their old normal. They rebuild themselves from the pieces of what they were before, and in the end, they're something different, but still whole and functional – even stronger. That's called post-traumatic growth. That's what I want for anyone reading this book.

Confidence

Remember in Chapter 4, when I said you need a toolbox of skills and abilities in order to achieve your goals?

Well, here's another one.
You need core confidence.

But confidence isn't the same as arrogance. A lot of arrogant people actually have what therapists call 'situational confidence'. Situational confidence is dependent on your surroundings. As long as you've got your buddies around you, or you're in a place you feel comfortable, or everyone is agreeing with you and laughing at your jokes, you feel confident. But the moment any part of that supportive environment goes away, you start to crumble. All your insecurities come back and suddenly you're wondering if anyone likes you at all, or if you're making an idiot of yourself.

Sound familiar? It should – this happens to many people every day. But it's also exactly what happened to me at the dinner party in chapter 1. I walked in feeling happy and confident, and started slowly falling apart as soon as the producers chastised me.

As long as you rely on situational confidence, you'll always be left consumed with self-doubt – or you'll be stuck inside your shell, afraid to try anything new in case you end up feeling like a failure.

What you really want is core confidence.

Before I went on *Married at First Sight*, I thought I had done all the work. I had read all the self-help books and been to all the seminars, and it showed. I was confident, outgoing and had plenty of dating options. I thought I knew who I was, deep down as a person. Sure, I had made plenty of micro changes in my life: I had been going to the gym, taking self-help courses, constantly growing and challenging myself. But at the end of the day, it's the macro changes you experience through massive adversity that really allow you to grow as a person. After my experience on the show, I'm a completely different person in how I think about things and react. I have so much more clarity on who I am, and I don't sweat the small stuff anymore.

The big, transformational moment for me was at the first commitment ceremony. When I broke down, I knew I had to open up and let the pain flow through me. I couldn't resist it anymore. I was pulled back to my default identity and forced to examine what I, at my core, believed I deserved. I was walking around acting so confident, but I had to consider whether, deep down, anything had changed. The answer was 'no'. Buried under all the bravado, there was still a little voice saying, 'Bullshit, you don't deserve to be here.'

I could have blamed feeling that way on many things – the producers who pushed my buttons and treated me unfairly, my partner who wasn't a good match. But the truth of the matter was, I realised I was screwing myself over and over again by reverting to my default state. I had been hiding behind my ego but, deep down, that high-school kid who never felt quite good enough was still lurking around inside.

I realised that while I had situational confidence – based on my specific circumstances – my core confidence still wasn't there yet. This is the type of confidence that comes from deep within and cannot be rattled, no matter what happens to you.

Social media and situational confidence

Today, it's possible to spend your entire life on the internet. Even when we're just walking around, we're scrolling through Instagram or messaging our friends on WhatsApp.

Social media is a huge contributor to situational confidence; all of those 'likes' and notifications give us a dopamine reward, creating an addictive cycle of external validation. Your social media success isn't coming from you – it's coming from your audience. You can be an Instagram star and still struggle deeply with your self-esteem – in fact, it's more common than not.

That's because social media doesn't build real confidence. If you're used to getting external validation from clicks and likes and follows and then it stops, it completely destabilises you. Think about the last time you texted someone and they left you on 'read'. I bet it really bothered you. When you're looking to other people to make you feel heard and seen, you can't handle it when they leave you hanging even for a minute.

The other problem is that social media doesn't teach you how to interact with people in real life. The skills you need to gain Instagram followers have nothing to do with what it takes to engage with a real-life person. You can see this problem through dating apps, where we're very comfortable messaging other people, but get very nervous when it comes time to actually meet them. We'd rather get that little hit of validation and fill in the blanks with our imagination than meet them in person and discover they don't live up to our idealised version of them. Plus, we don't want to take the risk that they might not like us.

People are now interacting so much in the virtual world that they're finding it increasingly difficult to interact in real life. During an interaction, you should be able to gauge whether you're giving your power away, on the one hand, or, alternatively, being overbearing or too forceful in your opinions on the other. But we are becoming so disconnected that more and more people are struggling to read social cues or notice the subtle differences in behaviour.

But, thanks to the internet, rather than taking the hard lessons that a real relationship has to offer, we can just create artificial ones that don't challenge us at all. As a society, we are simultaneously becoming more connected and more isolated than ever.

The whole concept of a long-distance relationship is actually becoming more realistic in today's society, because it can just exist on an exchange of validation.

Before the internet, people went about their daily lives and went to work, but they were more inclined to socialise in person. After they left the office or on the weekends, they would meet up with friends and family and experience that human connection. Whereas now, if people feel the need to socialise, they can do it quite happily from the comfort of their home. There are even some video games out there now that allow you to have a virtual boyfriend or girlfriend!

Skill-building challenge: social intelligence

To gain core confidence in social situations, you need to train yourself to pick up on other people's signals. To help develop social intelligence, I would encourage you to go and talk to three new people every day. Strike up a chat with the person behind you in line at the coffee shop. Ask a stranger for directions. Ask a co-worker how they're doing – and *listen* to their response. Be consciously aware of the dynamics in this interaction and try to gauge what they are thinking and feeling in this situation, to the best of your ability. You might even try journaling about these experiences. Then, you can tweak your approach in later interactions and see how this changes the reaction.

By doing this, you will gain more social experiences in a year than most people will in their whole life! Building a massive inventory of social references and learning pattern recognition is the key to developing a skillset that so many people lack: social intelligence.

Diagnostic challenge: your default identity

Many of us gain our sense of self from our surroundings. However people treat us, that's who we think we are and what we deserve. But to really gain core confidence, you need to build an understanding of yourself that comes from within. You need to become aware of your own strengths and weaknesses, your own quirks and special traits.

You need this self-knowledge for the inevitable moment when people turn on you. Online bullying is real and it's vicious. Overnight, I was seeing thousands of hate-posts about me on media stories. Without that true, internal sense of identity, you start to absorb those negative ideas about yourself, just as you were absorbing the positive ideas before. Very quickly, you start to wonder, 'What if everything they're saying about me is true?'

When people are saying hurtful things about you, you need to strike a delicate balance between blocking them out and just absorbing everything. You can block everything out that makes you uncomfortable, telling yourself, 'That's not me; they don't know what they're talking about.' It may feel like the healthy thing to do, but really it's just your ego acting as a self-defence mechanism. On the other hand, if you let that narrative overwhelm you, and decide that you are the person that others are portraying you as, you'll lose yourself.

You have to find the growth opportunity in that negativity. It's always possible to improve yourself, so is there any grain of truth in what's being said that you could take away and work on? That's the challenge. But in order to do that in a healthy way, you have to start with a strong sense of who you are: good and bad, weak and strong. And that requires you to come to terms with your default identity.

Your default identity comes from your core beliefs about yourself. These are thoughts and ideas that you've had since you were a child, often coming out of any traumatic experiences you may have had. Those experiences, and the hard lessons you learned from them – right or wrong, healthy or unhealthy – are living in your subconscious, influencing your everyday choices and aspirations.

Many of us believe we are victims of our own circumstances – 'I don't have that dream job because I don't have enough experience,' or, 'I don't have the money I want because I'm not good at saving.' The truth is, the only thing that stands in front of what you want is YOU! You are the number-one person victimising yourself and screwing yourself over. Often, this happens because we are addicted to our default state and our default identity.

So, how do we know if our default identity isn't serving us? Here's a great meditation exercise to help you determine this:

Close your eyes and imagine that you've just been magically transported into your body for the first time. Just like a body-switch: this is someone else's body, and you've just arrived out of nowhere.

How does it feel? What sensations are you experiencing? Is there any sense of unease? What is the experience like? Do you like your surroundings? Is it enjoyable to be in this body, or do you want to get the hell out? If you had to write down what it's like to be in your body, how would you describe it? Be really honest with yourself and rate what your experience is out of ten.

When I tried this exercise before getting on the show, my experience was a five out of ten. That's how I knew I had to dive deeper. Ever since the show ended, I have been on a journey to uncover my core confidence. The transformation has been far more drastic and permanent than what I went through to get situational confidence. I've seen more profound progress in the last year than I have over the last ten years combined. I want to see that happen for you, too.

The conscious vs. subconscious mind

If your default identity *isn't* serving you, how can you change it?

It starts with understanding what your subconscious mind does for you and how it functions.

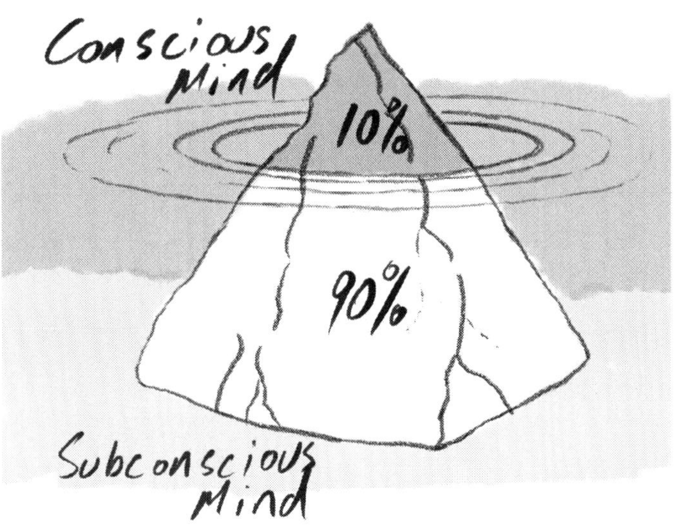

We all have a conscious and a subconscious mind. The conscious mind is everything that you're aware of right now in this moment, and the subconscious is the thoughts below the surface. For example, if you saw the reunion show, do you recall what colour my jacket was? You may not have been aware of it a second ago, but in a minute or two, the memory may resurface. That's because it was in your subconscious.

Some people compare the mind to an iceberg, where you can only see ten percent of the whole: the ten percent of your mind is the conscious thoughts above the surface, and the other ninety percent is the subconscious below.

The reason our minds work this way is so we can function and survive. If you had to constantly be aware of everything in your immediate surroundings, you would become overwhelmed by stimuli and lose your mind! However, the subconscious mind is also where we store our traumatic experiences and deep beliefs about ourselves — and most of the time, the two are deeply intertwined. Whether it's being bullied or family dramas, those negative experiences we have in our childhood are repressed into our deep subconscious. With them, we also store those negative beliefs about ourselves: for example, 'there's something wrong with me and that's why I was bullied.'

We never go back to question these limiting beliefs and, since the mind is repetitive, we play them over and over again like a broken record. If they're not dealt with, they become stronger over time and, ultimately, run our lives. As an example, think about New Year's resolutions. If someone wants to lose weight but constantly falls off the diet bandwagon, there may be a core belief in the subconscious that they can't lose weight because they haven't seen any evidence of it in the past.

Or perhaps they associate being overweight with their default identity. The same can happen with career decisions or staying in a destructive relationship.

To remedy this, you need to dig down deep into your subconscious mind and release your default identity. That means you have to forgive yourself for past mistakes, and let go of the things that happened that weren't your fault.

How can you possibly shake off beliefs that have been tailing you your whole life?

One strategy involves eliminating guilt and resentment. Everyone has a past version of themselves that they hate: maybe you got bullied and didn't stand up for yourself. To heal from these experiences, visualise going back in time to those moments and being kind to yourself. Remember that you did the best you could with what you knew in that moment. Give yourself a hug, forgive and move on. Remember, this isn't a one-time exercise; it's something you have to learn to do over and over again, every time these hurtful thoughts and feelings surface.

The next stage is a little more challenging! Holding onto resentment towards others can be just as damaging – it's a sign they still have power over you. So, imagine doing the same to the person who hurt you – for example, that bully who made your life hell. If you do this enough times, you'll eventually realise that you're no longer triggered by those feelings of guilt and resentment. That's when you know that you've moved on.

For me, this was something I needed to do with the commitment ceremony. While I blocked it out at first, I realised I had to go back and forgive myself for how I reacted at that point in time. In my case, that moment was captured on video and posted on YouTube, so to relive it, I just needed to find the video. Over and over again, I would relive that moment and visualise myself going back there and forgiving myself for that breakdown. Now, when I go back and watch the commitment ceremony, I'm no longer triggered by it. It no longer brings up those negative feelings. I've let it go.

It can be difficult to go back and revisit those traumatic memories, but once you go in and you're no longer affected by it, it no longer has power over you. That's the aim. That's how you'll know you have developed that core, unshakable confidence.

Chapter 6

Own Adversity, Earn Strength

Adversity is a natural part of life: that's just the way it is! Sometimes, you have to embrace the emotional drama, rather than run away from it.We were six weeks into the show, pretty much at the halfway point, and Blair and I started to hear more talk about the producers trying to force us to exit. The producers had given me some leeway after the breakdown because they saw some raw emotion and authenticity from me, but the storylines and stereotypes they'd dreamed up for us still came with an end date.

During production, airtime was everything. Every decision the participants made was about the amount of airtime they thought they'd get out of it. If you got airtime, that meant audiences would see your face and learn who you were. They'd come to know you and get invested in you. That was the kind of thing that could translate into fame and a new career later on, after the show aired. Many people on the show signed up in the hope they'd gain some fame out of it, build a new career and change their lives. But without airtime, you were invisible; none of the viewers would have a clue who you were. If that kept up for the whole season, when production wrapped, you'd pretty much go back to your old life. A little more money in your pocket, but no fame to build on. It would be like you went through the whole experience for nothing.

So, most of the participants were locked in a fight for airtime. They had signed up for the show with the specific goal of becoming famous, and they were willing to play along with the producers to make that happen. Ryan and Davina, the main stars of the show, got a whole storyline playing out on each episode, with reveals about their characters and relationship. Blair and I, at the opposite end of the spectrum, were only seen in a five-second clip every other episode.

That's because I had reached the point where I wasn't going to fight anymore; not for airtime, and not to stay on the show. I was done trying to force anything. Since that first commitment ceremony and my breakdown, I'd come to understand a lot more about what was really going on behind the scenes of the show. I'd put together all of the pieces I mentioned in chapter 1: I realised that the producers had a God complex and were treating us like their puppets, that there was never any intent of actually matching people up, that the commitment ceremonies were a lie, and that our sole purpose as human beings on the show was to play into the stereotypical roles they'd assigned to us.

Once I saw everything clearly, I decided to let go of my hopes and plans and open myself up to whatever happened. If they came at me with their fear and intimidation tactics to force me to exit the show, I'd just give them what they wanted and not fight back like I did before. That's how I got pulled into their vicious mind games and ended up breaking down. But now, I realised it was like a relationship. If they didn't want me there, why would I even want to stay?

Sure enough, one day the producers came into our apartment, ordering us to leave. They said all the same things as the first time: 'There's no point in you staying – nothing's going on in the relationship.'

By that time, I had rebuilt enough mental strength to be able to stay above the fray. When they started in on me, I just said, 'Look, I'm sick of fighting with you. I've been fighting with you from the start and I haven't seen this kind of pressure or intimidation put on any other couple.' I agreed to leave. Blair and I weren't in love, but we got along and didn't have any drama; that's what the producers meant when they said we had no story.

But Blair wanted to stay. She had left her job to join the show and she probably still had hopes that she'd get airtime and a storyline before it was done. I knew the main executive producer, Tara, was done with us and had no intention of giving us any airtime. But Blair wanted to stay, and that, technically, meant we both had to. A couple could only leave the show if they both wrote 'leave' during the commitment ceremony. This happens on the show every so often, where you'll see one person forced to stay on for several weeks because the other party wants to stay. But that's not what happened with us.

At the commitment ceremony, Blair wrote 'stay' and I wrote 'leave'. Afterwards, the producers were trying to figure out how to spin this in our storyline. Instructions came from Tara; I was supposed to go back on everything I said on the couch at the commitment ceremony and say I was in love with Blair. That would be our new storyline. Except it completely went against my integrity. I told them, 'I'm not going to say that. I'm not going to say I'm in love when I'm not.'

Tara's response was, 'Well, you can just leave the show now. We'll give you an out.'

I said, 'Don't we both have to write "leave" for us to leave the show?'

Tara said, 'No. There's no point in you guys hanging around.'

I couldn't believe how casually she said that, and with no fear of consequences at all. Every time I thought I understood how fake everything was on that show, they found a way to surprise me. Nothing about the commitment ceremony is real. The participants have no input whatsoever. Every decision, every development is dictated by these manipulative producers, drunk on the power of shaping public opinion.

Well, if you watched the show, you know we left the following episode after the commitment ceremony. And I left with my head held high, after all that bullshit and being singled out over and over again. I learned the lesson I went there to learn: how to bend in the face of adversity, but not break.

Learn to surf

You can't stop the waves, but you can learn to surf. – Jon Kabat-Zinn

This quote really captures what I believe about uncertainty and adversity. It's not worth your effort to go out of your way to avoid any failure or risk, ever. If you try that, you'll end up unfulfilled and resentful. Instead, I believe you just have to be willing to let the turmoil take over.

If I'd turned down *Married at First Sight* because it might go wrong, I would have missed out on a huge opportunity. I knew it might not go how I wanted, but I took the opportunity anyway because I could tell it was a chance to learn something new about myself.

So often, we hold back from taking chances in life because it might not work out. It's much more powerful to say to yourself instead, 'I'm going to do this because I think there's something valuable here, and I'm okay with wherever this experience takes me.' If you do encounter some chaos or adversity, allow it to change you until you get broken down, and then you can build yourself back up stronger than ever. Part of the reason I was able to do this on the show was because I had done it before: I'd overcome learning challenges in school, and I'd overcome limiting beliefs about what kind of career I could have. I'd then gone on to achieve the kind of income and lifestyle I never could have dreamed of as a kid.

Overcoming adversity can happen on a micro or macro level; it doesn't all have to be huge life-changing experiences. A micro example of overcoming adversity would be finally asking out the guy or girl of your dreams, and they turn you down. Or perhaps you ask your boss for a pay rise and they say no. You have to let that experience sink in and embrace both the negative and positive emotions that come out of it, allowing it to give you new insight into yourself. On a macro level, you might encounter something like losing your job or getting turned down for a promotion that you had your heart set on.

Big or small, there's always a lesson you can learn, and often, those little lessons can build into much bigger ones – like my difficulties with studying for my electrician's exam. But I think one of the biggest examples of adversity anyone can go through is public shaming.

After the *Married at First Sight* reunion, I started getting a tidal wave of abusive messages on Instagram. I was flooded with comments accusing me of being this or that. Even though I knew none of it was true, it was difficult to resist the urge to doubt myself.

What happens when you're in the public eye is that online trolls swallow the narrative that TV producers create. You get thousands of people hate-following you, flooding your social media to tell you what a waste of space you are. It's so easy to get sucked into it yourself. Even though it doesn't make sense, even though at first you know they're wrong, there are just so many comments and they're all so certain they're right. After a certain point, you start to absorb their thinking, almost against your will.

This happens often with people who have been publicly shamed. The groupthink narrative takes over and you begin to question whether they're right. You only have to look at Sophie Gradon, the 2016 UK *Love Island* contestant who sadly took her own life, to see how tragic the outcome can be. Honestly, I don't know how producers sleep at night knowing they destroy people's lives this way.

My example is an extreme one, but we've all been through this on some level. Whether it's online bullying, unflattering photos and stories being spread about you, or former friends dropping you, public shame is becoming more and more common thanks to the rise of social media. It's a challenge we all face to one degree or another.

What's interesting about public shame is that it's a direct attack on your sense of identity. We each have a narrative we tell ourselves about who we are, and you'd be surprised how much it depends on what the people around us think of us. When opinions turn against us, all of our surface beliefs are stripped away. For most people, especially if it's the first time this is happening to you, what's left is crippling insecurity.

To get through it, you have to recreate your own narrative based on your core values, and allow that to override everything else. To learn what your core beliefs are, ask yourself this: when you take away all your past beliefs and how people perceive you, what do you really care about? What are you still focusing on? These are your true, core values. For me, these were contributing, expanding, and helping people.

This is what I was doing for those six weeks on the show. I was reminding myself what I really wanted and what I didn't. When everyone around you is competing for airtime and a storyline and fame, it's so easy to get pulled into the fray and start to value these things you never cared about before. But that wasn't who I really was or why I signed up for the show. I just wanted to take on a new challenge, and maybe even meet someone. When I reminded myself of that and reconnected with my values, like my integrity, it became so clear what I needed to do. It was like all of these conflicting beliefs and insecurities and possible choices crystallised into just one mantra: *They can do whatever they're going to do, but I'm not selling my soul.*

That's how I got through the experience of the show itself, but I still wasn't prepared for the aftermath. When strangers who don't even know you are going out of their way to abuse and humiliate you, that's a whole new level of adversity. Thankfully, there was no film crew to capture what that was like for me. But I promise you, it was one the toughest things I've ever gone through.

When you go through this kind of traumatic experience, it can be helpful to think of it in terms of the five stages of grief:
1. Denial and isolation
2. Anger
3. Bargaining
4. Depression
5. Acceptance

Keep in mind, most people don't go straight from one stage to the next. We bounce back and forth, sometimes experiencing multiple stages in a day or even an hour. The goal is to try to get those moments of acceptance to last longer and longer, until they slowly become your default state.

As they say, whatever doesn't kill you makes you stronger. A huge part of me had to die after that reunion. You want to hold on to those old beliefs about yourself, but you can't resist what's happening. The adversity is changing you. You've got to let it take you through that dark place, so you can come out the other side a different person.

Once I accepted what I was experiencing, I was able to make clear decisions about how to deal with it. That's how I decided to go on a journey to explore who I was and what was really important. After that experience, I'm a lot more centred than I used to be. There's a lot less caring about what other people think and trying to adjust myself to fit into their reality. These days, I'm firmly centred in my own reality and have far more focus and clarity. I no longer get nervous about public speaking or social engagements, because the experience burnt away all the self-doubt I had before. That's the goal of going through adversity – that you'll come out on the other side stronger and wiser.

If there's a scary opportunity you know you'll grow from, you have to take it. No matter what happens in the end, you'll know you ended up in the place you were supposed to be.

Chapter 7

Get an Abundance Mindset

Most people have one of two approaches or mindsets to life. These are called the scarcity mindset and the abundance mindset. Which mindset you have determines how willing you are to take a risk, how confident you are in relationships, even what your career path looks like.

If you remember my story about the first commitment ceremony, that would be a pretty good example of a scarcity mindset. But not all of my time on the show was like that. As the weeks passed, I was working on myself and getting better at handling the ups and downs of life on a TV production set. There's one day in particular that sticks out as a day I had an abundance mindset.

After the reunion, the crew was scrambling and needed to schedule an additional day of filming. They wanted to backdate it to that six-week period between the final vows and the reunion. The filming was to get more context on the relationship.

At that point, Tracey and I were getting along fine, but obviously I was already starting to have some issues because of the inconsistencies I was seeing in her behaviour. But I pushed that aside and just tried to relax. We were filming at a beach, then in a restaurant with a quick wrap-up at the end, so I was ready to have a good day of filming. I had worked my way into a good position after the reunion in terms of my relationship with Tracey, and I felt like I finally had some leverage.

The production team came in the morning and started going through the text messages that Dean and Tracey had been sending each other. Now, if I'd had the same mindset I had at the start of filming, that could have really got under my skin. I'm sure the production team were hoping that, when they brought up the texts, I would get insecure, jump in and have a go at Tracey. But I let it go. I was feeling secure in our relationship, happy for once with my storyline on the show, and I wanted to respect her privacy. I chose to believe what she told me – though, looking back, I imagine they were having some kind of relationship.

Later that day, I remember asking one of the main producers about another character, Troy. When I asked how his filming was, the producer smirked and said, 'It's TV gold.' They always gave out this sense of enormous arrogance, because they had the full picture, and I felt like I was scraping around in the dark trying to piece everything together. Again, I could have let that moment get under my skin. I could have started worrying about Troy's storyline and whether there was some huge scandal happening there. A remark like that can wreck your day when you're on set. When you're trapped in the make-believe world of reality TV, it changes how you perceive things. I'll be talking about that in following chapters: about the rationales you start to adopt, and why you make some of the decisions you do.

But, instead, I honestly didn't really care. I was with Tracey, my storyline was getting airtime – things were going the way I'd hoped. Our relationship was going well at that point, so I was confident and honest all the way through the filming, which helped keep me grounded.

In the end, the filming didn't match up with what Tara had in mind or with the final reunion edit, so they scrapped it. But I always remember that day whenever I'm trying to explain what an abundance mindset feels like. I felt almost untouchable, like I held all the cards. Unlike that first time, at the commitment ceremony, I didn't feel scattered or insecure. There was no sense of trying to keep it together or searching for answers. I just was.

What is a scarcity mindset?

Scarcity is when there isn't enough of something. A scarcity mindset is when you believe that there aren't enough good things in life to go around: not enough love, not enough money, not enough success. It can also mean that you believe you aren't enough; not smart or funny enough, not likeable enough, not valued enough. Just like at the first commitment ceremony, scarcity can feel like a sense of insecurity, of searching for strength or answers, of fighting back your worst fears about yourself.

Sometimes we may have had childhood experiences that made us feel this way, and we still carry those scars with us; other times, a scarcity mindset may be a symptom of conditions such as anxiety or depression. When someone has a scarcity mindset, you can see it in their body language and the way they carry themselves. They tend to slouch and stare at the ground, and their pupils may even be dilated.

When you have a scarcity mindset, you don't believe that good things will come your way or that things will turn out all right. Anything in your life that you enjoy, you're afraid will be taken away. When it comes to friends, family and romantic partners, you need constant validation from them that they really love you.

I often see this scarcity mindset manifest in relationships. In a partnership, there's often one person who's more invested than the other. The less invested person often holds more power, because they're more prepared to walk away, and they both know it. Meanwhile, the person who is more emotionally invested in the relationship is terrified of losing it and is giving up their power to try to keep things together. They're constantly seeking validation from their partner, which can put a lot of pressure on a relationship. Once you get into this kind of mindset, it's a losing battle and can be very difficult to get back onto an even keel.

I saw this later on in my relationship with Tracey, after *Married at First Sight*. How much each person is going to invest in a relationship is determined early on, and it's built off the boundaries you put in place. With Tracey, I set boundaries right at the very beginning. She seemed to be more invested in the relationship, so I felt I had more power, so to speak. Of course, in this particular situation, she ended up betraying me – which goes to show that with pathological liars, you never really know if you're seeing their true personality!

What is an abundance mindset?

The opposite of scarcity is abundance. An abundance mindset, like the one I had on that last day of filming, is when you have the sense that there's always enough to go around in the world, so you don't have to fight for your share. You feel grounded and see the world through your own eyes – you're not constantly trying to read other people and guess what they think of you. People with an abundance mindset have a quiet confidence, thanks to their in-built sense of power. They don't allow small things to faze them. You can see that they're happier and more centred. There's a calm in their eyes; they don't give off a sense of fear or discomfort, as people with a scarcity mindset sometimes do.

Most people are naturally inclined more towards one mindset or the other, but sometimes you can transition between them quickly. Just think of a time when you started your day with a great mood and encountered a few obstacles. By the end of the day, you had probably entered a negative thought loop, your old emotional baggage was starting to surface, and you were trying to do anything you could think of to feel better. Often, scarcity mindsets are tied to substance abuse – whether it's alcohol, drugs or just overeating. People with a scarcity mindset are desperate to make themselves feel better with whatever quick fix is close at hand. Fortunately, you can also move yourself from a scarcity mindset to an abundance mindset. That's what I've done through my personal journey over the past few years. It takes time and effort, but it is possible, and I hope this book will help you on that journey.

You can see examples of people with both abundance and scarcity mindsets throughout past seasons of *Married at First Sight*. Davina Rankin is someone who appears to have a great sense of abundance. Despite being absolutely smashed by producers, she carried herself with grace and ease throughout the entire process. Having put herself out there as a model and on other reality shows, she had the deep sense of confidence that comes from overcoming adversity.

On the other hand, Sean Donnelly, who was matched with Jo, appeared to be coming from a scarcity mindset of fear and anxiety. He had a deep-seated belief that he was never good or attractive enough to hold down a relationship. When you have these kinds of limiting beliefs instilled in your psyche, it cascades into how you carry yourself and relate to others. Without healthy boundaries, you let people walk all over you, and that's what happened to the other Sean.

My journey from a scarcity to an abundance mindset

Throughout the years, I've slowly transitioned from a scarcity mindset to an abundance mindset. Before I went on *Married at First Sight*, I thought I had it all figured out. And on the outside, maybe I did: I had the job, the money, the girls, and I was travelling the world. But deep down, I was still harbouring the limiting belief I wasn't good enough.

Then, I went through a trial by fire by going on the show and copping endless abuse. I lost friends and family through that experience. I could have let the ridicule and name-calling eat me up inside, but that dark time became a turning point in my transformation. I had been running on ego, like many people do, and the show exposed my blind spots; weaknesses about myself I couldn't see until they were literally broadcast on TV. With my ego shattered, I had a chance to dig deep into my subconscious, pull out those deeply buried beliefs about myself and get to the root of my issues.

I've since been able to release those inner demons I've had since I was a child. Now, I no longer struggle with anxious thoughts. I'm more grounded and this flows into all aspects of my life – including the respect I demand from others.

How to know if you have a scarcity mindset

Here are a few quick tests you can use to determine if you have a scarcity mindset.

1. *Do you often feel the need to try to escape your feelings?*

If you find that you're engaging in escapist behaviours like drug or alcohol abuse, compulsive shopping or watching excessive amounts of pornography or Netflix, this can be a sign that you're operating from a scarcity mindset.

2. *Do you find yourself constantly going on social media to compare yourself to others?*

This is something that can be both a symptom and a cause of a scarcity mindset. If you're addicted to social media, it may be a sign that you need to meet others' expectations in order to feel okay. Over the years, on social media, we've developed a set of conventions around what kinds of behaviours get rewarded, so it creates the perfect reward system for someone with a scarcity mindset, who needs to meet external expectations and get external validation.

At the same time, social media can also create a scarcity mindset where there wasn't one before. Everyone online is posting a highlight reel of their best selfies, most beautiful vacation shots, greatest achievements, and funniest jokes. The more you expose yourself to this artificial fantasy of other people's lives, the more you may start to feel inadequate yourself.

3. *Have you ever taken a step to move yourself forward – a step that your friends and family weren't too sure about?*

When you're living for yourself, you will eventually do something that catches other people off guard. No one likes change, including your friends and family. And when you start making changes, your loved ones might not understand what you're trying to achieve.

When you start to enact meaningful change in your life, it upsets the status quo in all your social circles. It makes people question themselves; it shines a spotlight on the things they never accomplished. For that reason, very often when you are trying to really change, people around you may get uncomfortable.

By the same token, if you've never done something that surprised or confused your friends and family, something that made sense to you but not to everyone else – something like quit an addiction, leave a stressful job, start a healthy new relationship, make a major career change, go back to school, start a business, move to a new city, commit to a personal transformation of your mind or body – it might be a sign that you're not taking enough risks, and you're prioritising others' comfort over your need to grow.

How to achieve an abundance mindset

To move yourself into an abundance mindset, you have to reconnect with your deep passion for life and follow what you were put on earth to do. An abundance mindset comes when your life and commitments are aligned with who you really are.

We often develop a scarcity mindset because we've lost touch with our calling, drive, or purpose in life. This leaves us feeling unsatisfied without knowing why. Over time, the feeling of restlessness grows, and can cause us to adopt self-destructive behaviours.

In our subconscious minds, we value the input of our friends and family more than we realise. Often, our core decisions in life come from a place of wanting to please the people who raised us. However, when we try to please other people, we don't always get the same treatment back. So, we end up harbouring resentment towards others, and hating ourselves for it.

When you're constantly trying to please others, you're not putting yourself first. Even though others may praise us for being so 'unselfish', the truth is, it's not sustainable. You only get one life and you have to live it for you. If you choose a partner or career to please others, the longer you stay in it, the more dead inside you'll become.

What makes it worse is that traditional models of parenting, like that philosophy of 'children should be seen and not heard,' can teach people at a young age that their opinions and ideas aren't worth listening to. When we carry that belief into adulthood, it limits us, because we've never been taught to listen to ourselves and we're not prepared for others to take us seriously. That makes it all the more likely that we'll end up living for others. But you only have one life, and you have to live it for yourself.

To unearth your passion and find your true values, here are some questions to work through:

1. *What excites you?*
2. *If you had a year left to live, how would you spend it?*
3. *If you could do anything on earth, what would it be?*
4. *What do you do in your spare time if you've got nothing else on your plate?*
5. *If you had no job obligations or bills to pay, what would you spend your time on?*
6. *What would you happily do for free?*
7. *What used to make you feel alive as a kid?*

As an example, when I was a teenager, I wanted to be a rock star. I would spend hours in my room with the speakers cranked up, playing Green Day on guitar and singing along. I felt most alive and passionate when I was doing that. Later on in life, I asked myself how I could unlock that feeling again. I may not have become a rock star in the traditional sense, but public speaking and teaching and captivating people is how I access that passion.

People often don't follow their dreams because they think they can't make money from it, but you just need to get creative, be prepared to take a risk, and adapt. Try not to get too specific with your goals at this point, because it can block off other opportunities. Instead, imagine what your ideal life would look like, and work backwards from there. That's exactly what I did when I decided that I wanted a high income, and learned that a job in the mines would get me there. Your calling doesn't have to be exactly what you wanted to be as a kid, but you may be able to translate it into a sub-niche that you're still passionate about that can make you money. As long as it makes you feel alive and excites you, you're on the right path.

Another great way to uncover your passion is to do what the Stoics called a 'negative visualisation'. Considering your own mortality in this way can really kick-start the process of putting those plans into action.

It's basically a process of coming to terms with the fact that you are not going to live forever, by visualising scenarios where you lose loved ones, family members, even your own mortality. Systematically taking the time to reflect in this way can help you appreciate the moment, and also take action on the things that you really want in life; so when you look back, you don't have any big regrets about the things that you should have done, the missed shots and opportunities.

Abundance is about investing time and energy into something, because you then place value on it. Commit to something you're passionate about and follow it with an unwavering, burning focus. What's the worst that could happen?

Many of us believe we're going to live forever, which is why we stick to social norms and don't act on our dreams. We think we have all the time in the world, but the years fly by quickly – especially as we get older. Every day we spend trying to please others and live up to their expectations is one day less we spend living through our own intentions and following our passion.

If and when you achieve an abundance mindset, you'll know because your body language will change. You'll be able to see it in photos; others will comment on it. You'll have that calm in your eyes, that sense of being centred and approachable. Others around you will enjoy and appreciate this new energy, and you'll have a chance to rebuild some of those lost friendships and relationships on new terms – not to mention building new connections as well.

Chapter 8

Social Conditioning

Social conditioning is the process of teaching us social and cultural norms to guide our behaviour. It's what we're doing when we teach small children to share their toys or not to hit each other; we're conditioning them to behave in ways that our society deems acceptable.

But social conditioning isn't always a good thing. Sometimes it stands in our way. Sometimes we even find ourselves acting in ways that are self-destructive or hurt others, because it's what we've been conditioned to do.

From the very first gathering after the first dinner party on *Married at First Sight*, any time when the group was together for filming, we reverted back to high school. The floor manager was meant to facilitate the timing of the interviews and structure of the night, but instead of using normal language to convey his message, he acted like Joe Pesci from *Casino*.

If anyone were to ever-so-slightly step out of line, he would put his foot down and go straight to the power frame. A frame is simply a perspective – a way you present yourselves to others. This floor manager would present himself as the scariest, most powerful person in the room.

One night, we had just wrapped up a long, exhausting dinner party. We were ushered into the cocktail room at 3 am to be individually interviewed. These interviews are for the voiceovers used throughout the show. The producers purposely schedule the interviews at the end of a long day of filming because they know you'll be tried and probably a little drunk. It's the best time to get you to say something you never normally would.

Have you ever noticed that when you're in a new environment, maybe when travelling or giving a presentation in a client's office, all your senses seem a little heightened, like you're noticing more than you normally would? That's what the producers were counting on when they segregated us backstage – that the unfamiliar environment would put us on high alert, we'd get uncomfortable and start acting out. This happened throughout every dinner party and commitment ceremony.

In one instance, Troy went to sit down on a couch, and we all heard a crack as he sat down. The floor manager, old Pesci, heard it too. He gathered the whole group of us and bit our heads off. 'If you guys can't handle your fucking drink, we're going to cut you off and get you kicked out of the dinner party. You will be sent home.'

To be fair, the floor manager probably had no idea what he was doing. He just knew by breaking his rapport with us, and using the power frame and dominant tonality, he would get our attention. But he didn't understand how people's minds work. Humans have evolved since caveman days, but every message we receive still gets filtered through the more fundamental level of our brain: the reptilian brain or 'croc brain' as Oren Klaff calls it in his book *Pitch Anything.* Any new message that you get from your surroundings gets filtered through your croc brain to determine if it's a threat. If it is, your brain goes on high alert.

So when old Pesci started yelling, our croc brains snapped into action to assess if he was a threat. We were already experiencing fear of being singled out, and shame, since he was acting like we'd done something wrong. So that played into our social conditioning not to speak out in a situation like that.

They brought on experts to make the show look credible, but these 'experts' actually played a very minor role. I spoke to John Aiken maybe once, for about ten minutes, during the entire show. Most of the time, we only saw them at the commitment ceremonies. The experts were fitted with earpieces and instructed on what to say and how to say it. When taping, there'd be long pauses as they were talking, while they waited for instructions from the production team. Any actor could've done just as good a job – maybe even better.

So that left us at the mercy of people like old Pesci. I had one run-in with him myself, and this was during a futile attempt to use the bathroom during one of the dinner parties.

We were filming a dinner party, and they'd been supplying us with alcohol for the whole night, which often involved six to eight hours of filming. Obviously, when you've been drinking, you want to be able to use the bathroom. I went up to him and said, 'Excuse me, sir. Can I use the bathroom, please?' He said, 'No, go back to your seat now.' So I tried again about half an hour later: 'Excuse me, sir. I really need to use the bathroom.' 'No, go sit down. There's not enough time.'

By the time I made my third attempt, I was getting pretty irate, because you can actually get bladder damage from holding it for that long. So I said, 'Mate, if I don't go to the fucking bathroom, I'm going to piss my pants right now.' He said, 'What? Go sit down.' I said, 'No, I need to use the fucking bathroom.' He said, 'Go sit down.' Then he reconsidered and said, 'Oh okay, wait a minute.' And then, finally, he scurries me off to the bathroom.

He called me back fifteen minutes later. He thought it necessary to tell *me* to never use that language with him. Standing as tall as he could, with a dominant voice, he commanded me: 'Don't ever talk to me like that again.' I was annoyed just because it was so hypocritical. But it just goes to illustrate everything I've been saying about the filming process.

What made it so easy for them was that it was always a new environment for everyone who went onto the show. The producers were always in their element and we were always outside of ours. They had the situational confidence, the awareness of how things worked. They knew exactly what was going on behind the scenes; they'd been through this process before.

When you're outside your comfort zone, you fall back on your social conditioning to react to new situations. When people use aggressive tonality with you and speak down to you, most of us will instinctively do as we're told to avoid trouble. It's like when someone screams out, 'Fire', and everyone runs. It's pure reaction in the moment.

So, one cautionary thing to take out of this is to recognise when your behaviours or beliefs are a result of social conditioning, and work to change that and regain the upper hand.

Why we need social conditioning

You can see some of my own social conditioning in that story. Because of how I was raised, I wanted to try and live up to other people's expectations, even if they were delusions. Everything I did was meant to be 'cool' or to make me more popular. But that's not a value system. Social conditioning tells you how to act to please others, but it doesn't teach you about ethics, empathy or self-control.

Social conditioning is both a hindrance and a help. On one hand, we need it to get through life and function as part of society. With conditioning, we can learn patterns and behaviours from our parents and friends instead of having to figure everything out for ourselves. Those patterns teach us right from wrong, and show us what kinds of destructive behaviours to avoid. Without the strong influence of social conditioning, we wouldn't know how to get along with others or properly take care of ourselves.

But the behaviours we absorb through social conditioning aren't necessarily healthy or good for us. Just because we learn how to avoid hurting ourselves or others, doesn't mean we know how to live to our greatest potential. When we learn things in childhood like 'always behave yourself,' 'never raise your voice,' 'never be dominant,' it results in adults who go with the status quo, get the right nine-to-five job, pay their taxes and are always good little citizens.

You only need to look at kids to see the impact of social conditioning in action. Kids are so free. They're playful, running around, cheering and having the time of their lives. That is because they haven't yet been influenced by the societal pressures we're subjected to as teenagers and young adults.

The pitfalls of social conditioning

If you're not aware of it, social conditioning can slowly control you more and more as you go through life. From a carefree kid, you become a moody teenager and a depressed or anxious adult. You can always spot the people whose lives have been ruled by social conditioning. There have been a couple of older guys I've worked with in previous jobs who had clearly just let their lives slip by without doing what they really wanted to. They were angry, pessimistic and resentful towards everyone and everything.

Social conditioning has become even worse in the digital era, as people are constantly pinging off each other to gauge their reactions and gain validation. You put the content out there, it gets likes and comments, and you rely on that feedback to determine your identity and who you are as a person. Soon, you're posting selfies and vacation photos, not to show everyone what a good time you're having, but to get external validation to tell you you're having a good time.

There always needs to be a balance between fitting into a community – whether that's your friends, family or other kind of group – and asserting yourself as an individual. Because it's not enough to just live your life to please everyone else, and social conditioning will let you do that if you're not careful. As I've said previously, if you live your life for others, you'll end up feeling empty and resentful. So, at some point, you need to have a day of reckoning with your social conditioning and put it in its place.

How to break free
from social conditioning

In order to liberate yourself from social conditioning, you must go back to your core identity. Your values and beliefs, deep down, are the only things strong enough to help you override societal pressures.

The three things you need to understand in order to transcend social conditioning are as follows:
- *Who you are.*
- *What you value.*
- *What kind of boundaries you have.*

Let's start with who you are. I believe, in this day and age, most people don't have a strong sense of reality. They are constantly relying on social feedback, whether it be through social media or their environment. People are constantly looking to others to define who they are. However, becoming grounded in your *own* sense of reality is how you overcome social conditioning.

The same goes with our values. Back in the 19th century, people's value systems were a lot different than ours today. They placed a lot of value on family, integrity, trust and honour. These days, our value systems are based predominantly on consumer culture. In our global economy, we've been sucked into a vacuum of consumerism, and we place our values on things like having the nice car, a good watch, a flashy job or a hot partner by your side. That person may not even be your perfect match, but society places value on 'hot', so your values automatically align with that as well.

Personal boundaries are another important factor. If you go through life without having boundaries in place, people will not respect you or any decision you make about your life. It's like going to the gym to grow your biceps; you need to be consistently working and improving. You have to constantly reassess and ensure you're implementing boundaries, otherwise social conditioning will creep up on you and pull you back in.

In our society, in general, people tend to take the path of least resistance. We are inherently lazy. In our free time, we can sit down and binge-watch Netflix for eight hours. We like to 'go along to get along'. We're all naturally vulnerable to groupthink theory, which means we let society and government dictate how we think, feel and act. But if you don't make your own mind up about what you believe, other people will do it for you. So you have to get in the habit of questioning whether you're living up to your core values and beliefs, or just doing what everyone else wants. Because pleasing others is not the same thing as living life from your own core values.

I'll say it again – if you don't decide what you believe and stand for, others will do it for you. That's why you sometimes see rich trust-fund kids who have everything in their lives handed to them, but who are mentally weak because they haven't gone through any real mental adversity. One benefit of going through trauma or life experience is that it really tests you, your beliefs and everything you are as a person. This makes you grow very mentally strong, giving you a foundation to challenge groupthink and social conditioning. This is why some trauma survivors go on to become leaders and activists. They become so firmly grounded in who they are and what they believe that they're able to provide a sense of certainty and purpose, not only for themselves but for others.

I've also found that going out and having new experiences after *Married at First Sight* – travelling the world, experiencing different cultures – has helped me overcome my own social conditioning. Experiences like that help broaden your perspective and allow you to see the world through your own eyes, rather than through the lens of what people have told you to see.

This is one of the reasons travel can be so great for developing yourself. It's not all about beautiful vacation spots and getting the perfect photo. When you experience other cultures and see how other people live, it allows you to see some of your own social conditioning that you weren't even aware of. For example, if you visit a country that's less consumerist than ours, you'll suddenly see your own materialism more clearly than ever before.

Chapter 9

Routine is Key

We humans are creatures of habit. We like our daily lives to have a sense of order and routine to them. These routines can be extremely powerful tools for self-improvement. If you can create a routine around going to the gym, or eating healthy, or meditating, or anything else that helps you, you can completely change your life.

That's what I learned in the summer of 2015, during my stint as a signal technician in the Pilbara.

Working outside in the summer in the Pilbara, you've got two main problems to deal with: the heat and the flies. Temperatures ranged from 45 degrees Celsius all the way up to 60 degrees on the rail track. The work I was doing was hard manual labour – you are down on your hands and knees, removing rodding that drives the point machines so the switch can be changed out, doing up several nuts and bolts, adjusting the switches. There are only one or two signal technicians out at a time, compared to the entire track maintenance team I was used to when you're replacing sections of the track. And most of the guys I was working with were veterans of the trade with ten years' experience or more. Quite a few were brought over by a South African subcontractor company, and many of them had served in the military because it was mandatory until recently. So they had army training and were used to the conditions of getting up early and grinding hard for that twelve-hour shift.

Every day, we were up at 4.30 am, ready for a 6 am meeting and then out to the track. We had a designated car, but I always shared because I was a trainee. You'd grab your esky full of ice because, with that intense heat, you wouldn't be that hungry, but you could get through 10 litres of water on really hot days. Within minutes of stepping outside the car, your shirt would be drenched with sweat, and we had to work out there for hours at a time because there were limited windows of time in which we could do the work. The heat was unrelenting, there was no shade anywhere, and the flies were worse; you'd be covered with them, crawling over you trying to find somewhere to hide. It was like something out of an apocalyptic movie.

You can imagine how exhausted you'd be after twelve hours of that. It would be easy to go straight to bed the second you got back from your shift, and some people did. But I knew if I did that, I would lose all the progress I'd tried to make on improving myself. I didn't want my life to just be work and sleep for two weeks straight. I had worked my way back from a bad drinking habit and made fitness a part of my routine, which helped me set standards for myself. So I decided to make time for the gym every single day, right after my shift. My workout took up the time I would have normally used to eat dinner, so I'd have a protein shake instead and then go to bed.

The time I spent out there, doing hard labour in the crushing heat surrounded by some of the toughest and most disciplined individuals I've ever met, taught me a lot about the power of routine and discipline. Sometimes you're in a shit situation and you've just got to power through. But with the power of routine, you can cope with almost anything. Want to get something done? Add it to your routine. Need to get through a tough patch? Focus on your routine. Save your energy for the work.

Each and every one of us is a sum of our daily habits. We are made of routines. You wake up each morning, have your breakfast, go to the same job, see the same people and have many of the same thoughts. Often, these habits are so deeply ingrained that we don't even notice we have them. They free up space in our mind for more important things, because those core foundational habits – like brushing your teeth, getting dressed and driving to work – are done on autopilot.

It's only when our daily routines are disrupted, and we can no longer adhere to those habits, that we realise how much we actually need them. When you're thrown out of those core habits, it makes you submissive and reactive to anything that is thrown at you. I witnessed this firsthand during my time on *Married at First Sight.*

Micro v. macro habits

Before you begin working on implementing positive routines, you need to first understand that we all have both macro and micro habits.

Your macro habits are based on your identity and the beliefs you've formed over time. For me, a macro value is being a person of integrity. For you, it could be being a compassionate, empathetic or generous person. Micro habits are those activities you do every day, like having your morning coffee, doing meditation, or going to the gym. For me, a micro habit is getting up at 4.30 am to do a workout every day.

Your macro habits ultimately define your micro habits. For example, if you're someone who values integrity, you may be more likely to do what you say you're going to do, and hit your daily or weekly deadlines. Or if your macro habit is perseverance, you may be more likely to put in the extra 20 percent in the gym, even when it feels difficult.

Being so deeply ingrained, your macro habits tend to be more difficult to change than your micro habits. But often, to really stick to those positive micro habits, you need to first adjust your macro habits. The only way to really alter those macro habits is to take stock of your life and get some feedback from a trusted person like a mentor on where you need to improve your values and beliefs. The first step is being aware of the things you need to improve on in your life, so you can then recognise the smaller daily habits you need to adjust.

Starting a new positive routine

I'd like you to try thinking about your life in terms of your daily habits. If you have a particular goal in mind, or there's something about your life you really wish you could change, take a moment to measure that goal or change you want to make against where you are now. Take stock of your life and begin listing the ingrained habits that got you where you are now, good and bad. Ask yourself very honestly: 'How did I get here?' What daily routines and patterns of thinking have brought you to your current situation?

If you want something different for your life, those habits are going to have to change. You have to take control of your routine. So, now, envision your goal in terms of where you want to be six months from now. What milestones would you pass along that six-month journey? What things would have to happen for you to end up where you want to be? What daily or weekly habits would you need to put in place in order to make those milestones? Write it all down.

For example, I knew I wanted to write a book. I envisioned that moment I'd hold a copy of it – the moment it would go live on Amazon. I thought about the steps I'd need to take for that to happen; I would need a cover designed, and before that, a final manuscript. I'd need to work on each chapter, and before that, I'd need to have notes and materials – maybe an outline. I thought about the people I'd need to work with, the daily and weekly habits I'd need to have to work consistently on the book.

For example, let's say your goal is to meet your perfect partner. Obviously, one of the things that will have to happen is you'll have to go on dates with different people before meeting someone you click with. To go out on dates, you need to meet people. What habits do you need in order to meet people? Well, you need good social skills. You have to be comfortable talking to people you don't know well. Remember the example I gave in chapter 5 about developing an active practice of interacting with strangers every day to build core confidence? It isn't about a 'meet-cute'; it could just be a remark on the weather in an elevator or in line to buy coffee. But do that every day for a year, and there will be a noticeable difference in your social confidence. I've seen it in guys who have undertaken this practice; their body language has changed a little – maybe they're speaking a bit louder and clearer. They just seem more open and confident. This tiny habit can add up to a major personality shift.

How to maintain positive habits

It's a cruel irony that positive habits tend to be far more difficult to implement than negative ones! In order for positive habits to stick, they really need to align with your internal core values, or your macro habits. Of course, implementing positive behaviours is only half the battle – you need to actually stick to them long enough for them to become habits.

1. Schedule them

Health psychology researcher Phillippa Lally examined the habits of ninety-six people over a twelve-week period. Each person chose one new habit for the twelve weeks and reported each day on whether or not they did the behaviour and how automatic the behaviour felt. On average, it takes more than two months before a new behaviour becomes automatic – sixty-six days to be exact.[3]

This is why, when you first start exercising, you have to drag yourself to the gym in the beginning. But after a few months, you begin to see results. That positive reinforcement establishes that you're onto a good habit, which keeps the momentum going.

To make sure you actually stick to these new habits, it can be useful to schedule them in. I personally use my Google calendar to schedule my new habit into my morning routine and stick to it like it's a work schedule.

2. Get a mentor

Often, when people first start trying to adopt new habits, they find it too difficult and give up too early. This is why, when it comes to implementing positive habits and routines, it's important to

---

3   Phillippa Lally, Cornelia H. M. Van Jaarsveld, Henry WW Potts, Jane Wardle, 'How are habits formed: Modelling habit formation in the real world', Eur. J. Soc. Psychol. 40, 998–1009 (2010).

have a mentor. This is a role model and someone who currently is where you want to be. Having a good mentor helps keep you accountable, even when the going gets tough.

3. Make it work for you

Find ways to work this new habit into your existing schedule. It has to be something that works for you. That's the only way it will become truly part of your routine. For example, when I first started getting into fitness, I worked in a remote area and didn't have access to a gym. Instead of building my routine around going to a certain gym, which would have gotten disrupted when I went away, I downloaded a workout plan and got a mentor on board to keep me accountable. Having them there meant I didn't give up straightaway and, eventually, working out became a habit. Now, getting up at 4.30 am to do my morning workout is something I do automatically because it's part of my routine. I'll do it even if I've had drinks the night before, because it's part of my schedule and makes me feel 1000 times better!

Just because you might have a goal that others have, like getting fit, it doesn't mean you have to do it the same way that others do. If cardio workouts give you nightmares, find an exercise that you genuinely enjoy doing – maybe a dance class or yoga. If going to the gym makes you self-conscious, consider an at-home workout program or even a personal trainer. You can always branch out later, once you've got a solid foundation and some confidence built up. If you want to eat healthy but don't have time to shop for fresh food twice a week, see if there is a meal-kit service or online grocery store delivery that you can order. I do this, and it takes the emotion out of grocery shopping, so I end up making healthier, more rational choices.

This means you have to take some time to think about how you can create habits that work for you, instead of just trying to adopt the same habits everyone else seems to have. That's the best way to create consistency and make sure you're taking the right actions, or at least some actions, instead of procrastinating.

No guilt, no self-sabotage

Be kind to yourself as you set out to build a new habit. Accept that you will probably have setbacks at first, and set realistic expectations. If you want to change your diet, you probably won't be happy giving up your favourite foods and trying to eat the healthy foods you don't necessarily like but know are good for you. Instead, try to take at least one action per day towards that new healthy eating habit. Work on improving one meal at a time, like finding new healthy ways to eat breakfast. If your goal is to get fit and you only make it halfway through your workout, that's still better than nothing. Before you know it, if you keep that habit up over a few months, you'll have your workout on autopilot and you'll already have made progress.

If you're trying to give up a bad habit, you'll need to replace it with something. But you don't have to throw the whole habit out; keep the part that is actually good and can be healthy, and replace the part that is bad for you. This is an idea from *The Power of Habit* by Charles Duhigg, a Pulitzer Prize-winning *New York Times* reporter.[4] For example, if your bad habit is going out and drinking, you can still go out in the evening and have fun – just replace the negative part of drinking too much. Find a new activity to do instead; maybe hit the gym with a workout buddy. If you normally have dessert every night, you can still enjoy a treat after dinner; just replace the part where your treat is sugary and unhealthy. Instead, try a cup of herbal tea and a square or two of dark chocolate or a piece of fruit.

Work backwards from the goal

These small, positive daily habits eventually add up to those big, lofty goals. If you've got a goal you want to achieve in six months, you need to work backwards and figure out the little daily habits you need to take to get there. This is exactly what I did to write this book. I envisioned what it would be like to hold the book in my hands, then reverse-engineered the steps I would need to take to make it a reality.

---

4   Charles Duhigg, *The Power of Habit: Why we do what we do in life and business* (2011) https://charlesduhigg.com/books/the-power-of-habit/

Set milestones and rewards

Often when you set a big goal, you end up spending a lot of time beating yourself up for not making more progress. You don't see how far you've come – only how far you've left to go. But my mentors taught me to set milestones along the way to my goal and reward myself for each milestone. Plan out your rewards ahead of time, and make them meaningful and fun, to give yourself even more motivation.

The daily habits of successful people

There are a few daily habits that most of the successful people I know have in common. You may want to consider introducing these into your everyday routine.

1. They practise gratitude

Most of the world's big self-help gurus agree that waking up gratitude is a key to living a successful life. Tony Robbins has a video on YouTube that shares a morning routine with a range of breathing exercises and meditations. I have an old video from the '80s that goes through a seven-minute routine that helps you get into a state of gratitude. This helps you adopt a more positive outlook and focus on the things you do have, rather than what you don't. You can practise this by writing down three things you're grateful for each morning or night, or simply thinking them or saying them out loud.

2. They have morning routines

Having a morning ritual is one of the most important habits you can have, as it sets the tone for the rest of the day. Say you're running late for work and have a crappy breakfast; it sets the precedent for the rest of the day. So, you get to lunchtime and think, 'Oh, well, I've already had an unhealthy breakfast, so I might as well continue down that track.' This is why it's so important to start off right every single day.

Personally, I like to wake up at 4.30 am, get straight out of bed and do my twenty-minute morning workout video. Then, I hydrate, take a shower and am ready to tackle my emails and start my day. Doing this every morning ensures I'm coming from a place where I'm grounded, centred and focused, rather than just being reactive to anything that's being thrown at me.

If you follow any influencers on Instagram, you'll often see them sharing their morning routines. It's how they've gotten where they are. I'm a big fan of following inspirational people. Not so I can just be a spectator consuming their content, but so they'll inspire me to get up and take action to improve myself.

3. They celebrate their wins

When it comes to adopting positive habits, most people don't stop enough to give themselves a pat on the back and recognise how far they've come. They just move on immediately and start striving for the next big goal. It's important to reward yourself for the effort you've put in, as it's this positive reinforcement that keeps you going. Many of my mentors will give themselves a small reward whenever they reach a certain business goal or hit a monetary amount.

Recognising the positive habits they've formed is an important form of self-evaluation. The world's most successful people don't just drift through life. They're constantly taking stock of which habits are serving them and which aren't, rather than just getting stuck in their daily routines.

How to break out of a bad habit

What your life looks like today has been shaped by your daily habits. So, if you're overweight, that's likely due to a build-up of daily habits like overeating and a lack of exercise over the years. This happens when we don't put in the time or resources to set up positive habits; instead, bad habits have crept on in.

If you want something different, you need to take control of your routine and change those habits. Take stock of your life and see what habits you have instilled to get to the point you're at now. Ask yourself honestly, how did you get here? Which habits do you need to ditch to get to where you want to be?

Bad habits often stem from not having any boundaries in place and getting carried away. They can also arise from being in a rut and not seeing any change in your current situation. For me, it was going out and drinking all the time.

Often, you don't realise how bad it is at the time, until you look back on it a few years later. Drinking doesn't do anything to you overnight, but it can slowly chip away at your life and eventually leave you with nothing.

Many self-help gurus say that, in order to break out of a bad habit, you need to first create leverage for yourself. This is a strong motivation to escape a painful emotion, such as shame. It's the reason so many people get back in shape before a big event like a high-school reunion. For me, that leverage was looking at myself in the mirror after a long holiday filled with drinking and thinking, *Enough of this.*

I think many of us see the best results when we're put in a position of pain and are trying to get out of it. Project into the future what your life will look like if you continue smoking or eating junk food or drinking excessively. What will your life look like and what will it cost you? Escaping from this future pain can be a strong motivator to quit this habit.

I went to high school with a guy who was morbidly obese, and clearly had unhealthy habits instilled from his childhood. After being bullied constantly throughout high school, he decided to make a dramatic change in his life.

The first habit he introduced was going to the gym, and the second was getting a personal trainer and mentor. He enjoyed working with his personal trainer so much that he ended up studying personal training himself. He is now a qualified personal trainer and bodybuilding competitor, and his whole demeanour has changed. He's gone from a shy, reserved person to someone who is very positive and outgoing. This is the perfect example of someone who has used his pain as leverage to change his life.

Chapter 10

Conquer the Shadow Self

We go through times in our lives when we are fixated on certain goals. Then years later, when we look back, we can't even relate to those values anymore. We can see that those things we were so obsessed with had nothing to do with who we really are.

I was sitting in the green room in the Channel 9 studios one morning, waiting to go onto the *Today Show*. In the past, I would have been looking for the nearest exit to bolt out of because of my anxiety – that panic-stricken fear. But, instead, a wave of calmness washed over me. I was ready to tackle this opportunity.

I've come so far over the last decade with learning this skillset of overcoming self-defeating thoughts. And it is a skill. Just like any other skill, it takes practice and repetition.

One of the first big seminars I went to was in Las Vegas in 2010. The dating community had just come into its own, after the release of the Neil

Strauss book *The Game.* One of the main characters of that book had started his own company, and James, my friend from Brisbane, was one of the instructors for that company. He started working for them back in 2008. That's when I first met him in Sydney. We became good friends after that.

Before this trip, I had made sure I was well-prepared. I had watched all the online seminars; I was fascinated by social dynamics. I was pumped and ready to go for this much-anticipated trip. We walked into the conference room and I remember feeling the energy in the room. It was buzzing with excitement. I was sitting there, watching the speakers, thinking how engaging they were, that it was so entertaining, and that it really felt like they were there to help. I had this nagging feeling that I wanted some of what they must be feeling, up there on stage. I was sitting there thinking, *Could this ever be me? Could I actually go on stage, and not freeze, not be in my head, not be panic-stricken and shaking? Could I ever get over my fear of public speaking?*

At that point, I thought it would never happen. I could only sit there and admire these guys going up there with such confidence, displaying their authenticity in a way I'd never seen before. But they had learned it; after all, it was a self-development seminar. I know it was skewed towards dating, but it was literally about a bunch of guys who probably started out in the same situation as me. Who'd taken that step and overcome that fear, and learned that they could achieve whatever they put their minds to.

So, they gave me great inspiration. And, looking back, I was thinking, *Wow, I like this.* It really created a fire in my belly. I knew James could help me grow that fire.

Over the course of the next few years, James and I travelled around the world every opportunity we had. I joined him on his programs where he would teach self-confidence and dating techniques, and he would also run seminars every week in a different city.

I remember I got called up to speak in Perth. It was a very spontaneous invitation to join a tour, so I had no plan. My heart rate and adrenaline were running wild. I couldn't get over the past traumas that I had – those past beliefs and values I'd clutched onto, that I wasn't enough. That I wasn't able to do public speaking. That I wasn't smart enough to improvise a compelling and articulate speech. Sure enough, when I got on stage, it became a self-fulfilling prophecy. I froze and James could see me struggling. So he stepped in to help coach me through the rest of the tour and speeches.

It was one of the most nerve-wracking experiences and one of the hardest things I've done. It's almost the same fear mechanism that you get with the fight-or-flight response, where it feels like you're getting attacked. It's the same kind of emotions, and it overwhelmed me because I couldn't let go of those past traumas. I was still holding onto those deep shadow-self thoughts that I wasn't enough.

I remember doing videos with James. We used to do a lot of YouTube travel videos; I hated them. I'd always get this massive pang of anxiety every time I'd come up to do a video with him. I couldn't see past that huge emotional barrier about speaking on stage or on camera. It would overwhelm me every time. I kept telling James, 'There's definitely something wrong with me. I can't get past this.'

Until I went on *Married at First Sight* – that was my trial by fire. David Goggins, in his book *Can't Hurt Me,* talks about the idea of 'callusing' the mind. It's about using negative experiences to train your mind, just like you train your muscles – through repetition. I did exactly that, putting myself under intense scrutiny and going through my traumas one by one, burning away that past self. There was no other option. I had to let go of my past self for me to actually survive the challenges ahead of me. I couldn't fumble my way through the whole tour. I couldn't go on nationally televised shows and not be able to speak. It just wasn't done. So I had to find a way.

Those self-defeating ideas come from a specific source in our psyche. It's called the shadow self. If we ever want to be rid of them, we have to drill down to that core self and deal with it.

What is the shadow self?

We are all made up of two different sides, like the two sides of a coin. There's the conscious you, who's reading this book right now. Then, there's the subconscious you, otherwise known as your shadow self. This is the person you're trying to hide away, both from yourself, and from the world. This part houses those thoughts, emotions, beliefs and experiences that we deem unacceptable because they threaten our ego or our sense of self. We don't want to believe we have these thoughts; we don't want these memories. So we stuff them away.

Many authors have written about the shadow self, but one of the first was Carl Jung. He developed his theory from Freud's idea of the unconscious, the area of our mind where all of our negative repressed memories and emotions live. Like Freud, Jung believed the shadow self was an extremely powerful part of our psyche, but he believed it could also have positive aspects, such as strengths and truths we are not ready to accept, that could set us free and unlock our true potential. Jung believed if we ever want to become truly ourselves, we have to accept our shadow first.

If we go through a really traumatic experience, many of us will block it out and go, 'That's not a part of me; that's not my identity.' This happened to me after my breakdown at the commitment ceremony. Initially, I blocked it out and wouldn't accept it as part of my identity. I would think, 'That wasn't me; that wasn't me breaking down and crying like a baby in front of a national audience.' When we repress emotions or truths, they become part of our shadow self. They don't lose any of their power to hurt us; we just stop being aware of their influence, and we start spending a lot of energy trying to keep those ideas locked away.

Denying the shadow self

Many of us spend most of our lives trying to repress the pain and suffering we experience as a result of this split in ourselves, between the acceptable self that we can handle, and the shadow self that we can't bear to look at. We have all these unresolved issues deep inside us that are controlling us, and we're trying to escape from them and pretend they're not there. But if you're not aware of what's going on beneath the surface, how do you expect to make any kind of lasting transformation in your life?

What we do, instead, is constantly seek validation. People who live in denial of their shadow self take an outward approach to life. They use distractions like alcohol, drugs, partying or Instagram-likes to fill the void and mask their shadow self.

When I went on *Married at First Sight*, this was me. Like many guys in their thirties, I wanted fame and fortune – and what better way to get them than going on one of Australia's biggest TV shows? During and after the show, you become a mini-celebrity. There's literally a camera crew following you around. You're going to all these amazing events and getting VIP service; you're travelling and meeting all these influential people. I thought I had it all. Every day, every weekend, there was somewhere else to be, and it felt good because I was distracting myself. I was living in denial and relying on the external fame and attention to fix my internal insecurities. And it just didn't work.

But even when I was studying and improving myself before going on *Married at First Sight*, those efforts didn't work either. I wasn't addressing the real core issues hidden in my shadow self, so everything else I did, no matter how healthy it seemed, wasn't fixing the real problem.

Have you ever been on a holiday and, even though you were in a beautiful, tropical paradise, still felt shitty? Maybe you went with a significant other, and found yourselves having all your usual arguments? You changed your environment, but quickly defaulted back to your internal state, dictated by the shadow self that you may not have even realised was there. We can see this same behaviour in people who win the lottery. They spend the money on everything they've ever wanted to do, but studies show that they don't end up any happier than the rest of us. They have more resources to escape those internal issues, but as long as they're not addressing the shadow self directly, it will always be there.

Confront the shadow

Your shadow self determines your baseline – the default state where you spend most of your time. It's the source of your inner voice, for better or worse. If you can address your shadow-self issues at the source, it will open up a whole new dimension of the world for you. Your essential emotional state will change, and it will feel like you've never seen things this way before. Self-help gurus often try to give people a glimpse of this feeling by having them stand up, jump around, and show some excitement about life. That disrupts the inner monologue and gives a moment of relief. You might have a default state of feeling like crap, for whatever reason; old insecurities and traumatic memories could be creating a really unhappy baseline for you. But that can change; it's possible to get a new perspective on life and move the needle so that you actually feel awesome inside. I've done it, and the change is incredible. I'll explain that a bit more later on.

But I didn't get there by finding some magical new status symbol or partner who filled that void forever. I did it by learning that I could be enough just as I am. For long-lasting change, you have to make changes to your inner state, and that means confronting your shadow.

The true art of transformation is realising and acknowledging your deep-seated insecurities. Knowledge is power and it's only once we bring these to the forefront that we can really address and overcome these. To get to this point, you need to understand what's triggering you and what's causing these issues in the first place. It's really hard to get to, because your mind doesn't want to go to this dark shadow self. It's unpleasant and difficult.

So, how do you access this?

Work through your triggers

Your triggers act as a portal to your shadow self. A trigger is something that brings up a memory of a traumatic experience. Everyone tends to think of a traumatic experience in terms of someone going to war and getting their leg blown off. And, yes, of course, that's an extremely traumatic experience. In that example, veterans with PTSD will have triggers such as fireworks, because the noise sounds like guns being fired, and it brings up their memories of combat. What's so helpful about a trigger is that you can't ignore it. There are many unhealthy things that happen in our minds that we have no idea about, but a trigger grabs your attention and forces you to look at it. It's like a big red flag that something deeper is going on.

But it's not only violence that is traumatic. Being a kid and getting lost in the shopping centre is traumatic, too. Or being six years old and being shamed by the girl you like in front of the rest of your class. Why? Because it's too overwhelming for us to process, so we disown the experience completely. That's what creates the split between the shadow self and the conscious self. Those memories could be triggered by our emotions. If the trauma is getting lost in the shopping centre, the trigger could be you turning around and finding you've lost sight of the person you were with – you could start to panic, because it brings back that memory. If your trauma is being shamed and rejected by someone you like, the trigger could be anything that makes you feel that sense of rejection again, because it takes you right back to that traumatic experience and brings up all that pain like it was yesterday.

That moment at the commitment ceremony was a trigger for me. The producers berating me brought back painful memories from my childhood. At that moment, my instinct was to pull those feelings to the surface so I could learn from them. Later, I took myself through exercises to bring up those triggers again and again, using exposure therapy, and let myself accept that my reaction to that trigger was out of proportion to the actual significance of that memory. What happened twenty years ago shouldn't still be my reality. It was a moment in my life, and I needed to let go of it.

Often, when we're triggered and we're faced with these feelings again, resistance kicks in. The mind doesn't want to go there. We try to stuff those emotions down and pretend they're not there. It feels like that's what we need to do to survive, and maybe in that moment, it is. But in order for us to move on from the trauma, one day when we're safe and ready, we have to bring those experiences to the surface and let them engulf us, over and over again, until it doesn't hurt anymore and we can release them.

Question your shadow self

Another thing you can do to unlock those self-sabotaging inward beliefs is have a conversation with your shadow self. When these thoughts begin to bubble up, ask your shadow self *why*. Approach it from a place of curiosity, not hostility. So, if your self-sabotaging belief is that you're not good enough, ask, 'Why am I not good enough?' Replay the question and see what comes up in your mind. You might be sent an answer like, 'Oh, you never lived up to your dad's expectations,' or, 'You never finished your Master's degree.'

Take guilt, for an example. For people who have done something in the past and haven't let go of it, it will always subconsciously rear its ugly head and say, 'You don't deserve this.' Like, 'Remember how you used to bully your sister back in ninth grade?' or, 'Remember that girl you cheated on?' You know that these kinds of thoughts are self-sabotage, but you don't know which part of you is driving that behaviour. The answer is, it's all coming from your shadow self and the memories and feelings you locked away there. Being aware of this is the first step towards reconciliation.

Get to the other side

The only way out is through it. You have to bring up that emotion, sit with it, and release it. It's only once you do this that you can get down to your authentic self. That's what happened with me at the commitment ceremony. There were absolutely layers upon layers of resistance as I was sitting on that couch going through those emotions. But I had to dive deep and let it go. And I'm so glad I did, because one of the most traumatic moments of my life quickly became the greatest. My life completely changed after that moment. It was almost like magic. Health, career, money, relationships... it was like everything just fell into place.

I often look back to a year ago, and it feels like I'm a completely different person to who I was then. I look back on the things I did and said, and I think, 'That's how I used to think back then. That's how I used to operate back then.' It's been quite a transformation. Now, not many things bother me, and I also have these almost uncanny sub-communication skills. It's almost like a sixth sense, where I can see when other people are getting triggered, and why. It's really quite remarkable.

You can do it too. Start by asking yourself: 'Is my life authentic?' Or are you living a life of escapism, always running to the next distraction? So many of us aren't happy because we're chasing some made-up fantasy that we think we want, or we're running away from a trauma that we can't face. If you don't have a plan for yourself, someone else will, and you'll end up living up to external expectations.

Chapter 11
Relativity

Have you ever wondered why people act so irrationally on reality shows? It all comes down to the theory of relativity – social relativity, that is. At any given time, we're all constantly comparing ourselves to the environment around us. We're pinging off each other to determine what's normal behaviour and what's not. In a closed-off environment like *Married at First Sight*, you resort to relativity and make decisions that you wouldn't normally make on the outside world – but, in that environment, they make perfect sense.

I understand this because of my work situation. Working in the mines means flying away at the worst possible times for the people around you, and sometimes coming back to a shit-storm.

When you're away from your family and friends, you lose those reference points. Suddenly you're in a new situation, removed from your daily life. That helps you get to know yourself. It's hardened my resolve in a lot of ways. Things that seem like a massive obstacle tend to put themselves in perspective when you're away. I want that for you, too – to have that experience of walking away from your surroundings and gaining a fresh perspective on life. Sometimes, you can feel trapped by your social circles, by your family, your friends. You constantly find yourself thinking about their opinions and feelings rather than your own. I felt that way while filming *Married at First Sight*: trapped in the producers' world, seeing myself how they saw me.

Working away gives me the chance to ground myself and get back in touch with my sense of self. I get a new perspective to refocus my goals, focus on what's important in that moment, and notice the things that are causing issues and where I need to improve. It's invaluable. But it's not easy. People think that – they come up to me and say, 'Oh, you're working in the mines. You must be making heaps of money,' – but it's not easy money. It's tough being away from the people I care about. It's tough to leave your girlfriend or your boyfriend at a pivotal moment in the relationship. It's hard to just pick up your things and get going for another couple of weeks. But I believe if I stay the course, the outcome will present itself.

Writing this book has been a release for me because I get to bare all and be completely open. There is a freedom in this that is part of my path, and I have only achieved it because my perspective was changed so much compared to when I was filming *Married at First Sight*. Being in that world does weird and wonderful things to your mind and how you try to rationalise to yourself the decisions you make.

What is relativity?

In the theory of relativity, everything is relative – even when it shouldn't be. You're constantly comparing yourself to the other people in your environment: family, friends and co-workers. Your sense of what's normal and what isn't is mostly determined by what's considered normal in your circle. And not only that – once we figure out what is normal, we naturally want to be a little bit better. We want ourselves to come first.

You're making decisions based on your current environment, rather than looking at the bigger picture. Imagine a circle surrounded by other smaller circles. Then, imagine the same size circle, surrounded by other larger circles. It's naturally going to look bigger when it's surrounded by smaller circles, and smaller when it's surrounded

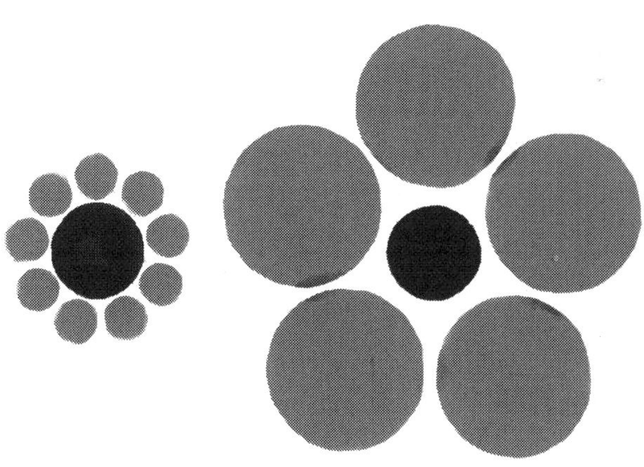

by bigger circles – but the actual size hasn't changed at all.[5]

This is just the way our minds are wired. 'We are always looking at things around us in relation to others. We can't help it,' says Dan Ariely, the author of *Predictably Irrational: The Hidden Forces that Shape our Decisions*. 'This holds true in both the physical and the environment that you're surrounded in, emotions, attitudes, and points of view. We always compare jobs with jobs, vacations with vacations, and lovers with lovers.'

The decoy effect

In his book, Ariely talks about the decoy effect. This is when you see two things or people with similar traits or mannerisms lined up against each other, but one is slightly superior to the other. Ariely calls the superior one A, and the less appealing one B, with the decoy of -A. Even if you have a tendency to settle in business or relationships, now that you have that option, you will feel certain on picking A. This is a sales tactic that's used to nudge clients into choosing the option you want them to choose.

Ariely uses the analogy of selling a house. If you were selling an upmarket house, you might have a decoy listed next to it on the website that needed minor fix-ups, but was going at a similar price point. Clients will pick the house that doesn't

5 Dan Ariely, *Predictably Irrational: The Hidden Forces that Shape our Decisions* (Harper Perennial; Revised and expanded edition, 2010)

need the renovations, every single time. Even if they wouldn't originally have been interested in either of the two options! This played a huge role in the choices that were made on *Married at First Sight*, as I explain later in this chapter.

Social pinging

We make comparisons not only in terms of material things and experiences, but also in a behavioural sense. So, we're constantly watching other people's attitudes, traits and demeanours. Then, we make a subconscious decision on how to act accordingly in that environment. So, for example, if you're at a VIP party, you may automatically feel like you have to prove yourself as worthy. You might carry yourself differently, try to be funnier or more impressive in some way. This is known as 'social pinging'.

Research shows we engage differently when we're faced with a different type of person, whether it's the victim, or the superficial Instagram girl. But often when we change our behaviour like this, we're merely basing it on stereotypes. We're using generalisations as a framework for how we expect others to act. And, in the same sense, the people who have been stereotyped are conditioned to act a certain way to enforce those stereotypes.

Ariely calls this 'priming'. You can see this taken to the extreme on *Married at First Sight*. The producers had stereotyped us as certain types of people before we even opened our mouths, and they used this to teach the others how to treat or speak to us. So, you had the loving father, the Instagram girl, the innocent type, the businessman, the party animal and so forth. Pretty much any stereotype you could think of, we had it in our series. As the show goes through, they're talking more about equality and diversity, but having a diverse cast of stereotypes really isn't what people are looking for. In my case, they had me down as the player, the womaniser.

Before every scene, the producer would ask us a certain set of questions to help activate those stereotypes. In my case, they would ask me a lot of questions about sex. With Davina, they would ask her a lot of intrusive questions to try to get a rise out of her and reinforce her antagonistic role throughout the experiment. And then you had Sarah, who they pinned as the marriage type, so they would ask her a lot of marriage-related questions, like, 'You and Telv are such a great couple. How long do you expect the relationship to last? Are you going to get married?'

Rationalising decisions on Married at First Sight

Along with the priming, the producers had also planned out characters for some of the characters they'd assigned us. Based on those, both Sarah and Davina were high-value characters: the hero and the villain. They got taken to lavish dinners, bought expensive jewellery, and stayed in the best hotels around Sydney. Meanwhile, for my homestay, we threw a BBQ and I had to pay for the food and drinks myself. The show never even reimbursed me. So it was obvious there were huge differences in how people were being treated, and with social pinging, we were all sort of noticing the new value system: drama and stereotypes got rewarded with air time and special treatment. Whereas I wasn't receiving any special privileges whatsoever, and it threw me off. It felt like a hit against my self-worth.

When I get asked about *Married at First Sight*, it's most often about the choices people made on the show. 'Why did you pick Tracey?' 'Why did Troy pick Carly over Ash?' Those decisions started with social pinging. The producers were treating us differently based on our value to the storyline – not our value as people. That created an uneven playing field where people who normally wouldn't seem all that appealing suddenly held a lot of power. That was feeding into the decoy effect; we ended up judging each other based on the value system the producers were using, not how we normally would.

That's where the decoy effect comes in. It's not just that there are two options and a third being the *Married at First Sight* experiment, with one being better than the other; it's also that we value those options based on our social pinging.

For example, Tracey isn't the kind of girl I would normally go for in real life, and neither was Blair. They're obviously two very different types of people, but when you line them up purely on relevance and social value on the show, Tracey seemed like a better version of Blair with the decoy of being evicted from the experience without playing any part whatsoever.

Tracey and Dean were getting the most attention from the producers, the most talk time and the most questions at the commitment ceremonies. That was what was valuable in that situation. Meanwhile, Blair and I were getting zero attention, and they just wanted us off the show. So, it was as though Blair was the decoy for Tracey, and as a result, I became interested in pursuing a relationship with her. All of a sudden, an option I would never normally have considered seemed very, very appealing! Once the relationship began, my feelings weren't a hundred percent there and I felt guilty, but I kept making excuses to justify my actions. This happens in relationships all the time; people get into relationships that they know will never work out, so they become defensive and try to rationalise the relationship even more.

You could see the same thing happening with Carly and Troy. In the real world, Carly probably wouldn't have gone for Troy, and vice versa. But Troy was the one getting all the attention, so he would have seemed like the A option, while her original partner, Justin, was the -A option.

Even though this all happened on a reality show, the logic behind our decisions was all true to life. In the real world, people stay in bad relationships out of a feeling of fear and scarcity, or they try to focus on the parts of the relationship that are good, when they know it's doomed to fail. You know you're going through this when your friends or family try to talk to you about your relationship and you get argumentative. That should be a sign that there are some underlying issues in your relationship. If you were on solid ground with your partner, you wouldn't even feel the need to argue about it.

A lot of people stay in a bad relationship because they don't believe they deserve that true partner they've always wanted. They've rationalised settling for something less than what they deserve. It comes down to low self-esteem and a lack of boundaries.

Why would any of us have had low self-esteem while we were filming on *Married at First Sight*?

The social experiment

The premise of the show was that marriage was an experiment, but they took it much further than that. They put a lot of pressure on us to perform, and there was no routine to help us stay grounded. As I've discussed earlier, we were at times short on sleep, and often drunk.

Just like me working away from home, it was an environment that removed us from all of our usual social supports. But where my work helps me stay grounded and put things in perspective, the producers added a bunch of extra pressure and curveballs purposely to keep us on edge. Because of that, we were all craving companionship and mateship more than you would in the real world. That's why you get such crazy scenes – people acting in ways they never would in their normal lives. It's a totally different environment, with stressors that most of us were unprepared for. There's an element of psychological trauma to it, especially when you emerge from that crazy environment. All you want to do is get back to normal and breathe for a minute, and then you find the footage that aired has been heavily edited to suit your manufactured character. Everyone thinks they know who you are now, and quite a few of them have it in for you. People who've been on the show have had to go to therapy afterwards.

What the mind thinks it deserves, it will get

Some people did come through the show okay. They were well-treated during filming, and mentally prepared for the aftermath when the show aired. That's because they already knew what to expect, which gave them some amount of confidence in knowing how to play certain scenes and get airtime. I think those of us who were new would do it completely differently if we were cast for the show again because, this time, we would understand the expectations and the processes behind the scenes that go into making the show.

Personally, if I could do it again, I wouldn't have held myself back at all. I would have been more myself, more up-front. I would probably have left earlier, because I knew things with Blair weren't going to work out and I should have said so. Instead, I held all those thoughts and emotions back, and it all came flooding out during the commitment ceremony. I was trying to filter myself for the show, like most of us were, and that's not what you should do. If you are in touch with your core values and know who you are, there shouldn't be any reason to bend over backwards to fit yourself into every new situation.

Just because a situation is new, it doesn't mean you have to let it break you down. When you're going through something you've never experienced before, and you're a fish out of water, you have to fall back on your own core beliefs and values – everything I've talked about in the previous chapters. When they say 'be yourself', what that really means is, you should release all those deep shadow thoughts that are holding you back. Give yourself permission to be enough, just as you are, and even your body language will start to show it. That's how you can start to find your confidence again.

I believe that reality shows should formulate the storylines after shooting has finished – rather than before. That way, producers could decide on storyboards and who deserves the most airtime based on the actual person, not on predetermined stereotypes.

Chapter 12

Turn to the Stoics

It was the night of the much anticipated *Married at First Sight* reunion. I was on my way to Channel 9 to do the live talk show, *Talking Married*. Walking into that studio, I had no clue that my life was about to change forever, and I would have a completely different outlook from that day forward.

As I was getting my hair and make-up done, I felt quite calm and collected. I got to see all the TV personalities walking in and out of the studios, which was rather exciting at the time. I was in good spirits and looking forward to the airing of the actual reunion. Little did I know, everything would change within a matter of hours.

As the airing of the reunion loomed, we were rushed into the green room so we could watch it before going on the talk show. I felt a sinking feeling in my stomach as I watched bits and pieces and realised how poorly I'd been portrayed. Instead of showing that I came to Tracey's defence and stuck up for her, they made me look like a jealous, psycho lover. It was almost amusing at the time, because it was the complete opposite to what had happened. It was so laughable that I remember thinking, *Nobody can possibly buy into this shit!*

Although I had to admit that my gold jacket looked slightly ridiculous, I just thought people would have a good joke about it and that would be the end of it. It wasn't until we were doing back-to-back radio interviews the next day that the magnitude of the situation hit me. As the interviews progressed, I became more and more anxious about how I had been edited. I was getting cold sweats, my hands began to cramp, and I could feel the tension in my neck.

Finally, it came to breaking point. We were in a taxi heading to Kyle and Jackie O's Haunted House at the Royal Sydney Easter Show, just after we wrapped up the interviews at midday. As I obsessively checked social media to see the latest reactions, the pressure mounted until, finally, I exploded. I started screaming at the cab driver, 'I need to stop. I need to stop.' It wasn't safe to stop, but I opened the taxi door and put my foot out onto the bitumen. As we travelled at speed towards the Harbour Bridge, I was ready to leap out.

When it was finally safe, the taxi driver came to a stop and I jumped out in a panic. So much tension, pressure, and anxiety were washing over me and I had no idea what to do next. I walked down to a nearby park and sat there for a good hour, contemplating my next move. As I sat on that bench, the philosophies I'd read in a book years earlier returned to me and, suddenly, took on a profound significance.

This book was called *A Guide to the Good Life: The Ancient Art of Stoic Joy* by William J Irvine. Stoicism is traditionally defined as being indifferent or devoid of emotions. Naturally, when I first read the book, I was opposed to this idea of banishing all emotions from your life. But I came to realise that it wasn't about banishing all emotions, only the negative ones that don't serve us. And in that moment of absolute emotional turmoil, this really resonated with me – because negative emotions are the source of all pain and anguish in our lives. To banish that would feel like an absolute godsend, especially with the traumatic experiences I'd had after the *Married at First Sight* experiment.

I now try to embody all of the principles of Stoicism in my daily life, and it's really helped me complete my transformation and improve my life. In this chapter, I'll take you through some of these core principles.

Negative visualisation

Conventional wisdom has always dictated that we shouldn't fret about the 'worst-case scenario' before it happens. However, Irvine says that, although it's uncomfortable to think about bad things happening to us, it can actually soften the impact if it does happen because we're more mentally prepared. He says that misfortune weighs heavily on those who believe nothing bad will ever happen to them.

In the case of *Married at First Sight*, I naively went in with the best expectations, believing I was going to get edited in a positive way. And, of course, when the worst-case scenario did actually happen, it impacted me so much more than if I'd visualised it beforehand. Psychologists Shane Frederick and George Loewenstein call this phenomenon 'hedonic adaptation'. It's when we get everything we desire in life, but move on to wanting the next thing, instead of taking stock and realising how far we've come in life. Their study was focused on lottery winners, and they found that most people from average backgrounds after winning the lottery felt the exact same way as they had before, just a few years later. They would start taking for granted their new Ferrari and mansion as opposed to their old, rusted Daihatsu and one-bedroom apartment. That's hedonic adaptation.

According to the Stoics, negative visualisation is the remedy for hedonic adaptation. They would periodically think about losing something they value, and that would make them appreciate it more. Of course, having all these negative visualisations doesn't mean you can just live in the moment 'YOLO'-style and do whatever the fuck you want. You still plan for the future and have your current goals and plans in action, but you also periodically reflect on the worst-case scenario, to become more grateful for the things that you have at this point.

Think of it as if your favourite restaurant was closing down and you were enjoying one last meal there. You would probably think it's one of the most joyous meals that you've ever had, the food was delicious, everything was immaculate, and you'd have fond memories of that. If you do negative visualisations and periodically reflect on the worst case possible, you'd probably appreciate life a whole lot more, too.

Dichotomy of control

The ancient philosopher Epictetus stated that, in life, there are three categories: things we can control, things we have some but not complete control over, and things we have zero control over. He said that the things in that first category – such as our values and the belief we have in ourselves – are what we should mostly concern ourselves with. In his book, Irvine calls this the 'dichotomy of control'.

On the show, the only things I could control were my own values and beliefs. And as much as the producers would try to manipulate us throughout the show to say certain things, I wasn't going to budge on these. This is why a lot of my comments got edited out of the show, because I refused to compromise those beliefs and values, and they didn't fit into the producers' narrative of me.

Then, there were the things I had no control over, like the editing process. Tara had a certain stereotype set out for each character and determined how much of a role they were going to play on the show before we even stepped on set.

As the ancient philosophers say, it's like a dog barking. Yes, it's annoying and you think about it in the moment. But you don't walk around three hours later still upset about the dog barking at you, right? The same goes for other people's opinions and misconceptions about you. It's outside your control, so why would concern yourself with it?

The other category is the things we have some but not complete control over. Epictetus' advice was that we should concern ourselves with these things, but we should not base our actions on them. So, I had some but not complete control over how I was shown after I'd come to the realisation that I was going to be edited out of the whole show. That's why I decided to go into the reunion and make a big statement.

But what I didn't fully grasp at the time was that I shouldn't base my goals on possibly being able to change someone's opinion of me. I should have asked myself, 'Do I really want to be portrayed like this, just to get back at Tara and the Endemol team who have no influence on my life?' I fell right into that trap. When it comes to those things you have some but not complete control over, you should first set your compass on those goals through your values and belief systems.

Dealing with insults

The Stoics have come up with some excellent practical solutions you can use to combat insults. I found this tremendously helpful last year when I was dealing with a barrage of insults, not only from people I didn't know but also from close friends.

Irvine's first strategy is to evaluate the source of the insult. Ask yourself, 'Do I value his/her opinion? Does it hold any weight with me?' If not, then the critical remarks shouldn't upset you. You'll find that, generally, people who insult other people all the time have deeply flawed characters, and as philosopher Marcus Aurelius says, 'Other than deserving our anger, they should deserve our pity.'

Another strategy that I personally like to use for dealing with insults is to make my response humorous and self-deprecating. So, if a friend calls me Ellen, I say, 'Yeah, I'm a way sexier version of Ellen.' Another strategy is to not respond at all. If someone gives me shit about wearing the gold jacket at the reunion, I just look at them with a blank face. It's like I can't even comprehend their comment, it's so far outside my reality. Usually, they fall straight into my frame and I have the power back.

Seeking validation

One of the most life-changing principles I got out of Stoic philosophy is how futile it is to seek out status and approval – especially from those whose opinions you don't even value. Aurelius said that, just as it's foolish of us to concern ourselves with what other people think of us, it's also foolish to seek the approval of those whose values we reject.

This was the case with Tara, strutting around the set with a black cape on – yes, a cape – like a superhero. Everyone was seeking the approval of this one person, to get on her good side. But the biggest realisation I had throughout was, 'Why would I care what this person thinks of me? Their values don't align with mine whatsoever, and their moral compass is so off, why would I concern myself with trying to seek their approval?'

Our goal should ultimately be to not concern ourselves with what people think of us but, rather, focus on our present situation. Irvine adds that, if we do this, we'll make the best of today and, therefore, enhance our quality of life.

Chapter 13

Perseverance

I believe perseverance is the key to being successful in any endeavour. When I think about perseverance, I think of my first job as a paperboy running around the streets in Brisbane. The job paid $7 per run and I thought, *You know, there's actually no point in doing this paper run. The money's horrible.* But my old man took me out the first couple of runs and said to me, 'No matter what the job is, you always see it through to the end. You always persevere and finish the job.' That's always stuck with me.

Even though the job only paid a minuscule amount, we would go out together and deliver every last paper on our run. We had opposing paperboys on our routes, and I would constantly see them dumping the papers either in a wheelie bin or behind the BMX track in the park. I learned a valuable lesson from doing that paper run – the importance of discipline and seeing the job through to the end. These are two things I've embodied throughout my life.

In my opinion, perseverance equals effort. A lot of people go, 'Oh yeah, effort. That's fine, I'll just try a bit harder.' But then you see those Olympic athletes and think, 'I could never do anything like that.' But it's those small, incremental, mundane tasks that athletes do that form their daily habits and, ultimately, lead to those remarkable achievements. It just comes down to showing up every day, putting in the hours, doing the same thing habitually, and getting the results.

When I first started my online app business, I didn't even know how to make an app icon, let alone how to create an app itself! It seemed so outside of my realm, like you had to be a coder or something. But, with perseverance and effort, I was able to get it onto the app store within a couple of months. It just goes to show that being fascinated by the process and continually putting in the work on a daily basis goes a long way.

So, how do you develop that grit and persistence? Well, it has a lot to do with passion and being completely fascinated with the topic or hobby. You've got to love it and stay in love with it. It's kind of like a relationship. At first, you're just getting a feel for each other, your ups and downs, and whether you have commonalities or not. Then, over time, you fall in love with the person's traits and idiosyncrasies. If you have that love for it and are able to stay in love with it, you'll be able to complete it. When I was creating the app, I knew it was going to improve other people's lives, and that strong sense of purpose kept me going even when things got tough.

Another key aspect of persistence is practice and a constant desire to improve. If you were an actor, you might say, 'I may never play a role perfectly, but I wanna try as hard as I can. I want to develop.' Or, an Instagram model might be constantly striving to make her Instagram photos better, even if she already has 100,000 followers.

Swedish psychologist Anders Ericsson has a theory about the role of deliberate practice. He says it takes 10,000 hours over ten years to become an expert in something. However, there's a big difference between just repetitively doing something for ten years, as opposed to doing thoughtful or deliberate practice, or working on a competitive level.

For example, I'm an avid gym-goer, and I've been going to the gym since I was eighteen. Now, that would equate to thousands of hours, but it wasn't necessarily thoughtful practice and it doesn't make me an expert. When I first started going to the gym, I was simply doing it to get in shape. I didn't really have a specific goal. Sometimes I would be deeply focused on my workouts, and other times, I would be listening to music or thinking about other things. On the other hand, someone like Arnold Schwarzenegger would go to the gym each day with the goal of working on one specific muscle for hours. He used to focus in on particular muscle groups to make them pop more if he felt they were lacking. He would probably be thinking about competitions and visualising that moment to focus in on that specific goal. That's a learned practice, and what you really need to strive towards to reach expert status in anything.

Chapter 14
Value

How do you face down a bully?

There are many ways, but one of the tools that I've developed over the past couple of years is knowing my value and the bully's value. Anyone can talk loud and be intimidating in the moment, but if you stop and ask yourself what they really have on you, often you'll realise you're the one holding all the cards.

Over the course of filming the show, I had taken a lot of shit from Tara. Most of the castmates had. But I'll never forget the last time I ever spoke to her.

Tracey and I were in Sydney. She was handling some media obligations and I came along to have a getaway of my own. Tracey had become one of the breakout stars of the show, thanks to the cheating scandal that the producers manufactured.

We arranged to meet some fellow castmates for dinner: Troy, Justin and Gabrielle. It was a great dinner. We had a good laugh and plenty of wine as we talked about the instant stardom we were all starting to experience. People were coming up to us to ask for photos, and Troy was in his element. He was so polite and kind with his fans.

It was a big night, so I had a well-deserved sleep-in the morning after. Tracey got up early to follow up on her obligations, and I got a phone call. It was Tara. She was very cordial for about the first two seconds. But I wasn't fooled.

'Where are you?' she demanded.

'I'm in Sydney with Tracey.'

Immediately, she started to go off. 'Why are you in Sydney? You and Tracey cannot be seen together. You cannot be out together. I can't believe you're in Sydney.'

What Tara was worried about was the fact that the reunion hadn't aired yet, and people didn't know about the partner swapping that occurred. It would only take one paparazzi to get a photo of me and Tracey to spoil the surprise. The only problem was, in that moment, I realised I didn't care anymore.

The tables had turned. Once the season aired, we started to realise the characters and stereotypes they had created for us. Obviously, I wasn't happy with my stereotype. But that didn't matter. Filming was done, the reunion was about to air, and there wasn't a thing any of us could do to change it.

So I didn't need to put up with Tara's shit anymore.

I let her have it. 'You edited me out of the whole show, Tara. What difference does it make if I'm in Sydney or not?'

No response. So I kept going, feeding it right back to her. 'I can be wherever the hell I want to be. You don't dictate where I stay. You don't dictate who I hang out with. Who do you think you are?'

She didn't seem to know what to say. Might as well go for broke.

I said, 'From now on... ' and started to list all the gripes I had with her and her management style. I ended with, 'You have no control over me anymore. The show's finished! I don't give a fuck about your events. I don't give a shit. You're not going to use me anyway, so it doesn't matter.'

She said, 'Well, because of your antics, you got into the reunion.' Like it was a favour she'd done for me grudgingly.

So I said, 'Well, of course, If you cut that out, it's going to make your show look absolutely fucking stupid, isn't it? It's not going to make any sense. It doesn't make any sense already, but it's definitely not going to make sense if you cut that out. So you have to put it in.'

I got it all off my chest – all those things I'd been brooding on while watching the show over the past few months. Tara had no response. I knew the game now and how it was played, and she knew I knew her power was gone. So she hung up.

I knew I wasn't going to get off scot-free, of course. The reunion episode could still be edited. But how bad could that be? I also had no media opportunities after the show, through the ongoing events and publicity that Channel 9 provided. But I didn't care. And I had been truly outcast from the very start; they had started the process assuming I had no value. So what was I really giving up?

That's the thing about value. You either have it or you don't, and it's immediately obvious who has it. Once you see that someone has no leverage on you, you can be bolder, more assertive, and more confident. All you have to do to access this inner superpower is ask yourself, 'Do I have leverage here? What kind of threats can this person make?' As you evaluate what the actual threat is, you'll find that core confidence to say, 'Yeah, they could do x, but I don't care if they do. I can handle it.'

Understanding value

What is value? And how do we place value on people? Well, it's usually in relation to status or, rather, their perceived level of status. A good example of this was every dinner party on *Married at First Sight*. As we went through the so-called experiment, different plot twists would develop, and the people involved in those were suddenly perceived to be of higher value. You could always see this in how we were seated at the dinner table. Those people who were of higher perceived value (that week) were placed in the middle, usually opposite each other so drama would ensue. Most of the attention would be focused on those centre stage, and the people off to the side were discarded throughout the whole dinner party.

What I did at the reunion was flip the script. When they could no longer use the storyboard they had in mind for me, they wanted me to just quietly come back into the reunion and ignore Tracey. So, what I did, as a big 'fuck you' to them, was go over and make out with Tracey, then plonk my ass down right at the middle of the table. This completely messed up their table settings, and it was free seating at the last dinner party. The point is, just because someone wants you to do something, doesn't mean it's the right thing to do. How someone else thinks of you also doesn't have to be the way you think of yourself. You are enough.

Finding value in conversation

How you approach a conversation determines what you will get out of it. If you only call people up when you want to get something from them in the most aggressive way, every conversation becomes a power struggle. If all you want is for someone to pay attention to you and make you feel good, your conversations will only ever be about you. If you have social anxiety and worry that every conversation is going to go poorly, that might become a self-fulfilling prophecy.

But when you've accessed your core confidence, you're not worrying about what you'll get out of a conversation, or how long it's going to take, or what the other person thinks of you. You can engage with the actual subject matter, listen to someone else's point of view, offer your own take, and actually get even more out of the conversation than if you started it with a view to how you might benefit. You approach conversations with an eye to how you can give and take.

But sometimes it can be hard to have those real conversations, the ones that are a true exchange of ideas. So here are some tips for how to spot opportunities to have a real dialogue.

Read the room

During any given interaction, a person is generally thinking four things:

1. *'Does this conversation relate to me?'*

If it doesn't have hold any significance for them, they usually block it out. They're generally thinking, 'When are they going to stop talking, so I can start talking?' If you start talking about the flower arrangements on the table, for example, and it doesn't interest the other person, they're probably just waiting for their turn to talk.

2. *'Do I get it?'*

If you're explaining something to someone and it clicks, they immediately switch off because they understand what you are talking about. Anything you say after that, they probably won't hear.

3. *'When is it my turn to speak?'*

This is the biggest one, and you see it in extreme levels with narcissistic people. These are the people whose eyes glaze over while you talk, or they even just cut you off completely and speak over you to get their point across.

4. *'Am I being tested?'*
They're wondering whether they're being tested on whether they understand the concept, and if they passed.

Most people believe this line of thinking will help increase their status by pleasing the other person. But, in actual fact, it generally lowers your status or perceived value. This is because it kind of kills the interaction, as you're not being present or authentic. You're just operating through a filter the entire time.

As the conversation continues, you also want to try to get a sense for the emotional state that person is addicted to. What does that person's ego and self-image look like? What are they trying to get out of the situation? Where are they going? What's their line of thinking towards this conversation or thread? What are their priorities?

One thing to focus on is their eyes. Do they look tense, or are they looking away? Or do they look happy, relaxed, and at ease? You can use this feedback to determine whether your approach is working and tweak accordingly.

If the person looks bored or is clearly just waiting for their turn to speak, maybe you need to change things up in your next interaction. Perhaps you need to be more present; keep your responses shorter, ask more questions, and let go of that attachment to finishing off what you were saying.

Also, bring some awareness to what you're saying and the intention behind it. Is it about you, or is it what you're able to give? Ask yourself, 'Am I saying this to impress? Am I saying this to improve the story of me?' You always want to ask yourself, 'Am I offering value? Am I present or am I being responsive to the situation?'

Check your mindset

This brings me back to thriving vs. coping mindsets. When someone is just coping, they're always trying to relate the conversation back to themselves and see what they can get out of it. They don't feel they can spare the energy to really think about another person's perspective. But when someone is operating from a thriving mindset, they're thinking, 'I'm good either way. This doesn't impact me. I can relax.' Instead of trying to glean something from it or relate the conversation back to themselves, they're just trying to provide value and improve the vibe. These are the types who appear more laidback and are willing to let the conversation flow naturally.

So, to shift your focus from yourself, the key is to detach yourself from the immediate worth of the conversation. Instead, try to get outside your head and determine what the context of the conversation is. What emotional needs are people trying to meet through this conversation? Because every time you do something that doesn't address one of their needs, or say something that's not appropriate to the context, you're going to inadvertently suck the value out of the conversation. Try to notice the reactions of the people you're having a conversation with. Put yourself in their shoes and ask yourself, 'What are they thinking?' 'What are they feeling?'

The idea is to stay authentic and stick to your boundaries, so you're both getting what you need out of a conversation without the underlying coping framework.

You'll find that when you're operating within this coping framework, it gives the conversation a negative vibe. So, instead of thinking with a negative mindset and playing the victim, you've got to go into every conversation with the intention of just making it feel better.

This exercise may seem simple, but if you practise and apply it on a consistent basis, it can change your life. So I want you to go out and interact with three new people today. It can even just be simply asking your Uber driver, 'How's your day going?' That way, you're sharing some good emotions and thriving instead of coping.

Recently, I met a celebrity. He greeted me with a warm, authentic and positive voice. 'Nice to meet you, friend.' In doing so, he solidified his godlike status in the way he carries himself and the amount of value he has. Hopefully, by using a couple of these pointers, you too will be able to solidify some of that status and walk into your next conversation with confidence, ready to share value.

Chapter 15

The Game Plan

It all starts with a spark. You have a vision of the person you want to become, your ideal self. What starts as a hobby turns into a passion; then, suddenly, it occupies most of your time and thoughts. This happened for me a few years ago when I first got into self-development. It stemmed from the adversity of a failed relationship, and the question: 'Could I have done more to rectify it?' I knew I didn't have all the answers, and recognising that was the first step. The spark comes from realising you can make a change in your life, having the passion behind what you're doing, and enjoying the process, too.

Gaining the base knowledge

We're all given opportunities to find this spark throughout our lives; it's what you choose to do with those opportunities that truly makes you remarkable. A great example of this is going on a reality show. Each and every person who gets selected is presented with a great opportunity, but not everyone is ready to take it. It just depends on your perspective, and how you choose to deal with it. You can whine and complain and play the victim about how you were edited, or you can use it as an opportunity to strive to be better. Being so exposed on a show like that can bring up a lot of blind spots, which you can then use as a vehicle for personal growth. But a lot of people go through the show and just try to stay relevant and cling onto that fame, instead of using it as a platform to follow their true passion.

The first step is having the base knowledge to recognise those blind spots and realising you have things you need to work on in your life. It's like a detective looking for clues. Having this knowledge is the key to finding your spark, but a lot of people don't know where to look. It all comes down to looking for opportunities and recognising your RAS (reticular activation system), which we discussed in chapter 1. Once you've found that base knowledge, you need to find your passion and drive behind it.

Finding the passion

One great way to unearth your passion is to listen to the people around you. They won't give you the answers to what you should do with your life, but they can give you the clues about the paths you may want to explore. When you're passionate about something, you tend to talk about it a lot. So, the people in your life can help you identify those common themes you're always dropping into conversation. For example, when I first started learning about different strategies for dating and social dynamics, I would talk about it all the time. So, the people around me would say, 'You seem to be really passionate about this; you should give a seminar!' A lot of people would brush off this advice, but it's important to be able to recognise this as a sign and take it on board, because the things that excite you aren't random – they could be your calling.

When many of us think about a 'calling', we think of professional athletes who grew up with a bat in their hands, or performers who have been playing guitar since they were five. But it doesn't have to be something like that, because obviously not everyone can be an athlete or rock star. So, if you're a naturally empathetic or caring person, your calling might be to be a nurse, or if you've always loved experimenting with fashion, it could be to become a stylist.

Creating the game plan

It's one thing to find your calling and have a vision of what you want your life to look like, but you need to actually take action to get there. This is where a game plan comes in. Things aren't always going to work out the way you want. Working towards your goals isn't always fun or pleasant. There are inevitably going to be times when you don't feel like doing it. Sometimes, it's going to be messy and awkward, or you're going to be too tired. But you need to show up consistently, even when you don't want to, and stick to your game plan.

Take, for example, this book. Putting myself under the scrutiny of the media and the public isn't necessarily going to be fun, but it's consistent with my calling. The process of writing this book has led to more clarity for me, and, therefore, I decided to pour all of my energy and spare time into it. I have a future goal, and I'm going to work towards it slowly and methodically.

To follow your dreams, you need to know that it's not always going to be a fairy tale, and sometimes you're going to fail. But it's all about keeping that end vision of yourself in mind, and putting in the work consistently. So, say, you're committed to not going out and drinking for a certain amount of time. It may be hard staying home on a Friday night when all your mates are out, but if you follow through, you'll reap the rewards. You'll feel better and more confident, because you remained disciplined and held yourself to a higher standard than most people do.

People often look at someone who is successful and think, 'Oh, that guy is just lucky or naturally talented,' and, yes, there may be some element of luck to it. But the majority of their success is from having a plan and sticking to it, day in and day out – no matter how tough it gets.

It all comes down to having that drive behind what you're doing. It's having a plan and taking the first step, which builds the momentum to see that plan through, cascading into your next venture. This terrifies a lot of people and keeps them doing things they don't want to be doing in life. But if you want to be in the 0.001 percent who achieve their dream, you need to feel that fear and take consistent action, anyway.

Chapter 16

Roundup

Do you remember where you were when you decided to buy this book? Do you remember what you were struggling with, or hoping for, that prompted you to try and improve yourself?

Many people have lost confidence in this modern world. Social media and the deceit and corruption we see all around us have made people more afraid than ever to speak up. But if we just keep reacting to the world around us and letting it define who we are, we'll spend our whole lives just spinning from one situation to the next, never taking control.

What I've tried to do in this book is give you a series of tools to use to re-centre yourself and take back control of your life. No matter what life throws at you or how much you might think all hope is lost, there is always a way out. It really is all about your perception; improving your life starts with realising that you can decide how to view your situation. Then, you just have to move past your initial assumptions about yourself and how your life 'should' go, reframe your situation and figure out your next step. The tools I've given you are meant to help you do just that: overcome struggles, reframe your perceived weaknesses, and turn them into strengths.

If I'd believed what the producers and the media were trying to say about me, this book wouldn't exist. I never would have written it. Instead, I've created a guide for you with practical tools to figure out where you are now, where you want to be, and what actions you need to take to get there.

Tool #1: RAS (Reticular Activation System)

If you can change your thinking from 'Why are they doing this to me?' to 'What can I learn from this?', you'll be able to bring your full strength and power to any situation. Your RAS works on the idea that what you focus on becomes your reality. Direct your focus, shape your reality.

This is also an important tool for achieving your goals. You have to clearly set your goal in your mind and create some visual reminders like a vision board or a note or photo in your wallet – something you'll look at all the time. Then, create a belief system to go with this goal; constantly remind yourself how much you can improve your life by working towards this goal. The power of your RAS will cause you to suddenly start seeing opportunities and means to achieve your goal that you never noticed before.

I like to put a laminated sheet with a goal or a call to action on my mirror, on my window, or inside my shower, so I can always see it. That's a good way to direct your RAS on a daily basis; otherwise, you get caught up with the daily grind of going on Instagram and get thrown back into reactive thinking.

Tool #2: Storytelling

Humans are born storytellers. Stories capture our imagination and our attention; through stories, you can get a new perspective on the problems you're facing, sell a product or give someone a snapshot of who you are in a relationship. Throughout history, the people who have had the most influence and captivated their audiences were those who knew how to tell a good story. And every good story has three elements: the situation – how things were before the story begins; the interruption – some sort of tension, drama or obstacle to the situation; and the solution – how the issue was resolved or any changes that occurred as a result.

To tell a good story, you'll need to practise, practise, practise. Know your hooks and learn how to use your tonality. For example, to tell a story about someone trying to establish rapport, you'll need to use a high-pitched, rising inflection, a bad door-to-door salesperson. This implies a need or request. A neutral tone is fine for everyday conversations and small talk. And to describe dominance, you'll want to use a low, sharp and downward inflection, which will sound slightly aggressive or assertive. Mastering these kinds of tonal variations will add incredible, subtle power to your storytelling.

For example, to establish yourself as an expert in a given field, have a short sixty-second flash roll memorised that you can call upon when you're telling your story, so people will see you as an expert in that field. The 'flash roll' is an idea from Oren Klaff's book, *Flip the Script*. If you're interested in learning more about storytelling, I would highly recommend reading it.

Tool #3: Core confidence

How do you get core confidence? Through trial and repetition. Practice makes perfect, but you can start small; if you want to be a public speaker, you can start by enrolling in public-speaking courses. Find opportunities to speak in front of people daily, whether it's many people or just a few. These will become reference experiences that can build confidence; when you take on a new challenge, you'll have these in the back of your mind to remind yourself, 'It's okay. I've gone through this before and I know I'll do okay this time around too.'

That was one of the benefits of a challenge like *Married at First Sight*. Though the experience was difficult in many ways, it also offered a ton of experience with speaking on camera. We got into a daily routine, to the point where I can walk on camera and my mind just clicks into action; I know exactly what to do. That's the confidence you get by building reference experiences.

Tool #4: Abundance mindset

Core confidence and an abundance mindset go hand in hand. Once you get your confidence up, you'll slowly start to build momentum towards reaching your goals, and then you'll start to see more abundant opportunities. You'll know that you've put in the work, and you'll have the confidence to try out for some of these opportunities, and that, in turn, will open up even more chances to build your success. It all starts with building your core confidence and transitioning to a mindset that there's always enough to go around, so why shouldn't you take a risk?

Tool #5: Routine

Once you get your inner mind sorted, it's time to start building the right routine. Now that you know what you want, you need to take systematic steps towards that goal that you've been working towards. So it's not just going to happen by focusing your RAS; your RAS must trigger good habits and routines – for example, waking up early, regular exercise, diet. You need a routine to help you prepare for those important moments when you need to be a hundred percent focused on your performance. One part of that routine should probably be cutting out alcohol, because drinking causes your body to release natural stimulant hormones to combat the depressive effects of alcohol. This, in turn, affects your nervous system, changing your feelings, emotions and behaviour, and the temptation then is to have another drink, just to get back to your normal default state. It's not just about using RAS to focus on the outcome you want; you also have to use routine to cut out anything that could hold you back. That's how you build discipline.

Tool #6: Resist relativity

'Relativity' refers to our social practice of constantly comparing ourselves to our peers. Whatever they have, we want that and a little bit more. It's called 'social pinging': using social media, we get these glimpses of each other's lives and then immediately compare it to ourselves.

This can create an obstacle when you set out to improve your life. Sometimes, our family and friends have our best interests at heart, but relativity means that once you start making changes and improving yourself, it will cause others to question themselves and that can lead to resentment.

So, the best way to move forward is to get yourself some opportunities to be off on your own and define your goals independent of others. Once you've set out your core beliefs, your goals, values and routine, it will be easier to stand firm when others question and ridicule you. You can use the power of goal setting and your RAS to stay the course.

Tool #7: Perseverance

Once you've set your game plan, complete with timeframe and specific actions for what you want to achieve, the key is to never give up. These tools are meant to help you maintain the patterns and routines you've set up, stay firm in shutting out the distractions you've identified, and carry out the plan. You know what you need to do. Now it's time to execute the plan, and don't let anyone stand in your way. Step by step, you'll build a life you never dreamed possible.

An important part of this is to set milestones and celebrate when you reach them. Some people will lay out a plan, for example, with weight loss, with celebrations and rewards set out for when they reach each of the smaller goals they've laid out. Hitting a milestone is also an opportunity to reflect and adjust. What resources or people do you need to get to the next milestone? In particular, I find that external mentors, from outside your family and peer group, are the best way to move ahead. As I said, sometimes family and friends can hold you back if it looks like your achievements might force them to question their own choices. An external mentor will only ever root for your success and keep you going.

On reality shows

In this day and age, many of us are still naïve enough to expect others to have our best interests at heart. But when it comes to your future and your passions, you've got to know when to say 'fuck it' and just take the plunge, because your life and future is in the hands of just one person: you! You have to look at the world through your own eyes and trust your own beliefs and faculties.

Reality show production companies are basically unregulated to this day. They take advantage of a legal loophole that they're shaping popular opinion on TV . So what I'd like in future is for the show to be treated as the business that it is. I want there to be a formal inquest into harmful practices on reality show sets. Because no one has ever spoken up about this.

According to the Fair Work Ombudsman, examples of bullying include:
- Behaving aggressively,
- Teasing or practical jokes,
- Pressuring someone to behave inappropriately,
- Excluding someone from work-related events, or
- Unreasonable work demands.

So, my hope for this book is to help people going through a similar journey who have experienced any kind of adversity; anyone who's looking for a change in their life. I hope this book has helped you to see clearly that not everyone you meet has your best interests at heart, and that's why you've got to equip yourself to build your own life how you want it. No one else will do it for you.

Final Word

I want you to know that just picking up this book means something. It means you took the first step towards your goals, even if it was just a small step. Right now, as you are finishing up this book and getting ready for the next step in your journey, is an important time to look ahead and start setting those goals. Do it now, while you have the momentum. If you haven't yet started using these tools I've outlined, get started!

1. Envision the life you've always wanted.
2. Ask yourself what it would take to get there.
3. Break that down into smaller goals and actions.
4. Decide the first thing you're going to do to kick off your journey!

References

Chapter 1

Pease, Allan & Barbara. *The Answer.* Sydney: Harlequin MIRA, 2026.

Chapter 2

Brewer, E. Cobham. *Dictionary of Phrase and Fable.* Philadelphia: Henry Altemus, 1898; New edition, New York: Bartleby.com, 2000.

Chapter 3

Cordock, Richard Parkes, *Millionaire Upgrade: Lessons in success from those who travel at the sharp end of the plane.* Chichester: Capstone, 2006.

Chapter 4

Belford, Jordan, *Way of the Wolf – Straight Line Selling: Master the art of persuasion, influence, and success.* London: John Murray Learning, 2017.

Chapter 9

Lally, Phillippa, Cornelia H. M. van Jaarsveld, Henry W. W. Potts, and Jane Wardle. 'How are habits formed: Modelling habit formation in the real world'. European Journal of Social Psychology 40.6 (2010): 998-1009.

Duhigg, Charles, *The Power of Habit: Why we do what we do in life and business* (2011) https://charlesduhigg.com/books/the-power-of-habit/

Chapter 11

Ariely, Dan, *Predictably Irrational: The Hidden Forces that Shape our Decisions.* New York: Harper Perennial; Revised and expanded edition, 2010.

Chapter 12

Irvine, William B., *A Guide to the Good Life: The Ancient Art of Stoic Joy.* Oxford: Oxford University Press, 2008.

Kahneman, D., E. Diener, and N. Schwarz (eds), *Well-being: the foundations of hedonic psychology* (First paperback edition). New York: Russell Sage Foundation, 2003.

Chapter 13

Duckworth, Angela, *Grit: The Power of Passion and Perseverance.* London: Vermilion, 2016.

Ericsson, K. Anders, 'Deliberate practice and the acquisition and maintenance of expert performance in medicine and related domains,' Academic Medicine, Volume 79, Issue 10 (October 2004): S70-S81.

Chapter 16

fairwork.gov.au

https://www.fairwork.gov.au/employee-entitlements/bullying-and-harassment#what-is-bullying

Printed in Great Britain
by Amazon

49502418R00113